AIR MODELLER'S GUIDE TO
WINGNUT WINGS
VOLUME 2

W W W . W I N G N U T W I N G S . C O M

FOKKER
EIII

ZDENKO BUGAN

THERE ARE ACTUALLY TWO WAYS THAT I USUALLY PICK A COLOUR SCHEME FOR MY MODELS, EITHER BASED ON THE FIRST LOOK ATTRACTION OF A REALLY COLOURFUL OR TECHNICALLY DEMANDING CAMOUFLAGE, OR I CHOOSE SCHEMES FROM MACHINES WITH A WELL KNOWN PILOT OR RENOWENED HISTORY.

The Fokker E.III doesn't offer us with many colourful options as It's usually overall beige linen, field grey or with surprising twist - beige wings with a grey fuselage. Consequently right from the start, I knew that I would select a colour scheme of machine that was flown by one of German aces. After reading very interesting book 'Mein Fliegerleben' by Ernst Udet, I was quite certain that it would be a model of his aicraft that I would like to have in my collection. Fortunately Wingnut Wings also found this an interesting subject and added his Fokker E.III 105/15 into the selection provided in their Fokker E.III (Early) kit.

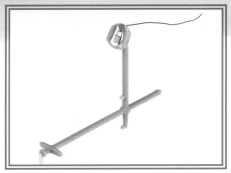
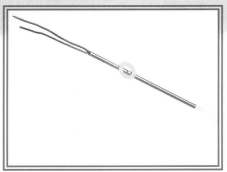
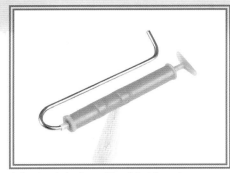

The Wingnut Wings kit contains parts for very nice and detailed model straight from the box. But as you know, there is always opportunity for additional aftermarket detail sets or a bit of pure scratchbuilding to enhance the detail. I decided to use the dedicated HGW photoetched set designed for this kit and enhanced a few tiny details in thr interior like the control column. All tubes, lines or pipes were replaced by brass tubes or lead wire.

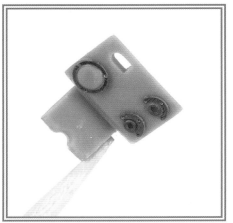
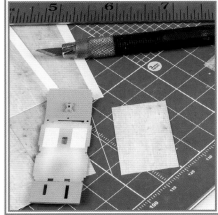

The simple Instrument panel details were also replaced by the nice photo-etched parts from the HGW set.

To create a good representation of wooden parts in the interior, I decided to use s wooden decals from Uschi van der Rosten.

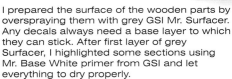

I prepared the surface of the wooden parts by overspraying them with grey GSI Mr. Surfacer. Any decals always need a base layer to which they can stick. After first layer of grey Surfacer, I highlighted some sections using Mr. Base White primer from GSI and let everything to dry properly.

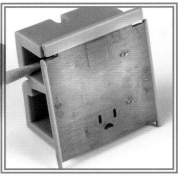
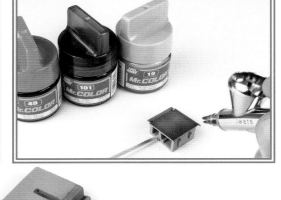

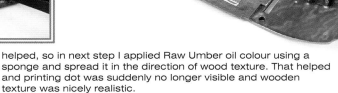

The downside of decals is the dot pattern of the printing process which can be visible under close examination. The next few steps were focused on minimising this effect. First I oversprayed the whole wooden surface with mix of Smoke and Clear Orange lacquers from GSI to darken and unify the look. It only partially helped, so in next step I applied Raw Umber oil colour using a sponge and spread it in the direction of wood texture. That helped and printing dot was suddenly no longer visible and wooden texture was nicely realistic.

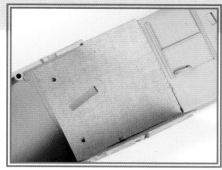

I decided to improve also interior side walls with some additional decaling. HGW canvas decals have nice linen texture, so I tried to use them as a base under the field grey colour. I wanted to make the final look more interesting, so I tried to do a bit of preshading under the linen decals with quite contrasting black colour, simulating oil stains that were quite common for Fokker

Eindeckers, only to find that HGW decals are completely opaque and not transparent at all. My whole preshading effort was completely useless. I had to take another approach then and sprayed postshading stains with mix of brown and black colour directly over the decal.

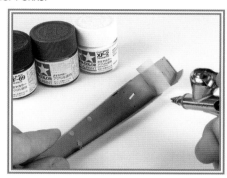

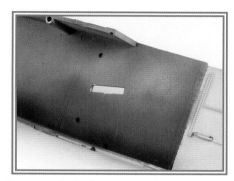

Finally the base colour layer was applied. At first I sprayed the middle tone - plain XF-22 Grey from Tamiya. Then I lightened it with flat white XF-2, spraying a few highlights close to the cockpit opening. With the opposite darker mix darkened with XF-69 Nato

black I sprayed some shadows into the lower areas. I was very cautious to not completely overspray the nice decal texture underneath, so it could show through the camouflage colour.

After everything was painted and assembled I started applying some simple weathering to the interior sections. The first step were filters. Today, all these products can be bought already prepared and ready to use but I prefer to create these from enamel colour diluted with white spirit. The mix is something like 5% of colour to 95% of thinner and it is applied by brush directly to the surface of model. This was also the case of my Eindecker interior. I created and used dusty, grey and darker brown filters and applied them one by one, after the previous one had completely dried.

All small details, corners and negative lines were enhanced by oil colour wash created from dark brown and black mix.

The most difficult part when painting practically any Eindecker is the representation of the special way its metal cowlings were finished. These were made of plain aluminum, and manually polished, which created "turned" squiggly patterns on the metal surfaces. Many modelers recreate this by brush painting but as these patterns were quite diffused, I decided that the only way to replicate them is to spray them using an airbrush. I tried to do this using an airbrush with a 0.2 mm nozzle using combination of GSI Mr. Metal Color metallic colours.

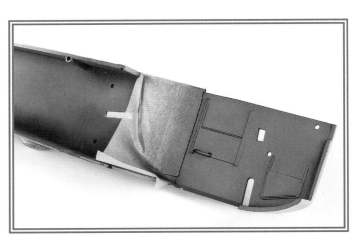

The base, darker layer was sprayed with Mr. Metal Color 212 - Iron, I just let it dry and did not polish it yet. That needs to wait for later.

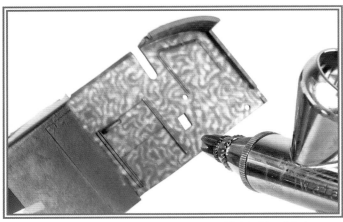

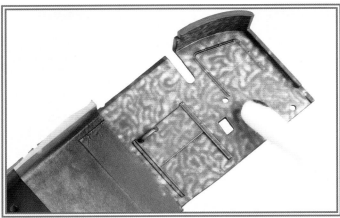

Then I sprayed little 0.5 mm thin squiggles with Mr. Metal Color 218 - Aluminum. I will not pretend that this is an easy job, it isn't! You will need some practice before working on the model. The pattern must be consistently thin, properly placed and the whole pattern not obviously repetitive. Of course I spent some time practicing it on the spare plastic sheet before I applied it to kit parts, and even then my hands were still a bit shakey.

if you give it enough time, you will eventually get it. Once it is all properly dried, you just polish the whole surface with dry cotton bud. Mr. Metal Colors from GSI can be polished, so that they start to look like real metal. You need to be quite soft while polishing the surface, if you push too hard, the pattern tends to be smudged into the darker background and you can loose the desired contrast in the overall effect.

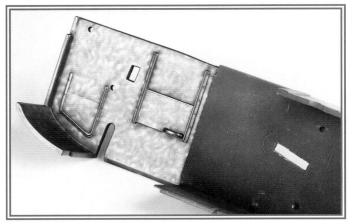

As you can see, final result is really worth the effort.

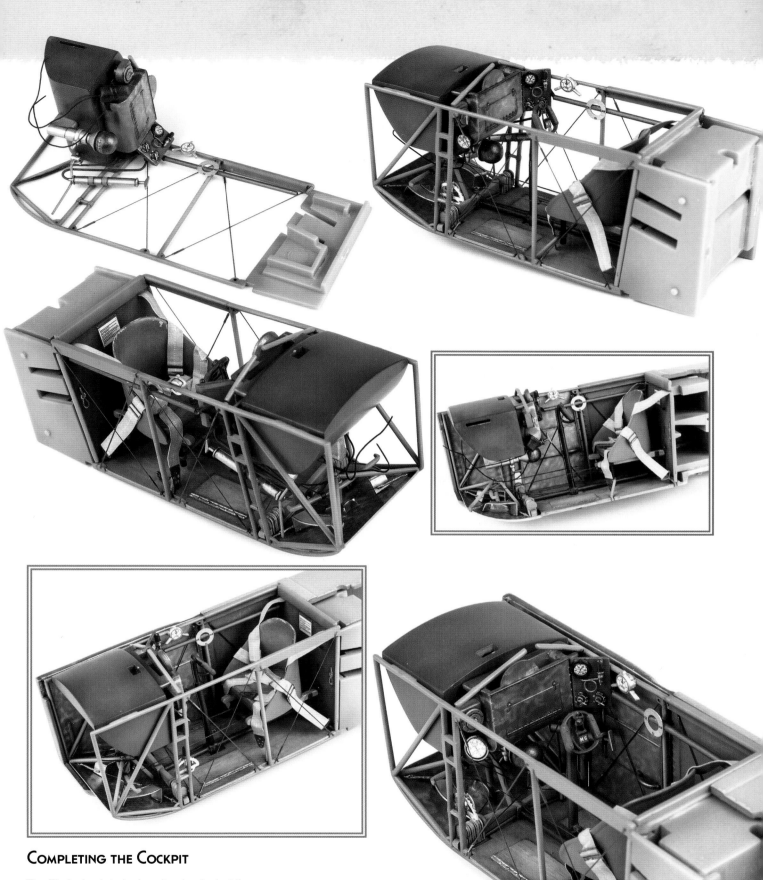

COMPLETING THE COCKPIT

The Eindecker interior is quite simple, but there are many
interesting details and material finishes to be represented. During
the final assembly I also changed the original photoetched
seatbelts for real textile ones from HGW. These drape realistically
like canvas, and can be shaped and glued easily. After some
simple rigging was added, I closed the fuselage halves.

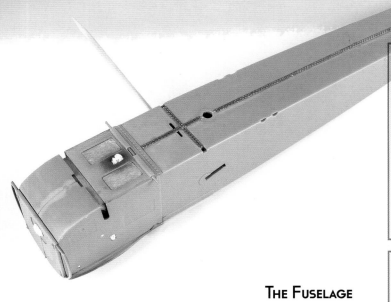

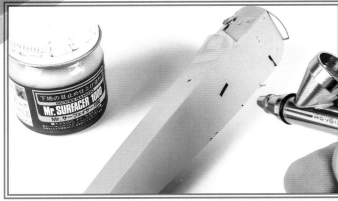

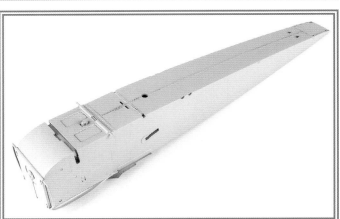

THE FUSELAGE

The HGW photoetched set also covers also some of exterior details. One example is the nice stitching on the underside of fuselage. You can be certain that I used it!

Before I started with any other painting action, the first step was the mandatory plain layer of Mr. Surfacer 1000. It will make ensure that no other subsequent colour applied will chip off the surface later, when you will start with aggressive masking or weathering.

After everything was dried and ready, I oversprayed the whole fuselage with base field grey colour. I used GSI RLM02, but it actually doesn't matter what color you use, as it is just a base for initial preshading. Any grey will work.

Then I sprayed preshading with really dark black and brown colours. This is to represent oil staining and dirt that was quite typical for Fokker Eindeckers. Rotary engines tend to spit and loose oil quite heavily and it travelled back down the fuselage to the back, mostly on the bottom sides of fuselage. As you can see, I used really dark and intense preshading, as you really can have a free hand here.

After you are satisfied with preshading, you can start applying the base colour itself. I used XF-22 RLM Grey from Tamiya for the whole fuselage canvas.

Because XF Tamiya colours are matt, before I applied the kit decals, I oversprayed whole fuselage with gloss varnish. It will prevent the decal edges silvering. Then the decals were applied with the help of reliable Mr. Mark Setter and Mr. Mark Softer and after everything was dry, whole fuselage was oversprayed with a matt varnish.

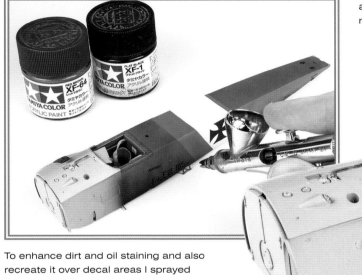

To enhance dirt and oil staining and also recreate it over decal areas I sprayed subtle irregular stains with mix of Tamiya colours - Flat Black and Red Brown, highly diluted with thinner.

In the same way I achieved the squiggly turned metal effects on the interior I needed to do this also for the exterior parts. Using the interior surfaces as a training area, the outer exterior panels are the real battle zone.

THE MOTOR

The Oberursel U.I engine supplied with the kit is very nice, but if you want to have the ultimate level of detail for the engine you can obtain a real gem, the Taurus resin Oberursel engine set. Its details are truly astonishing as you can see in the photos here. It will require some additional effort to be assembled, but it really is a standalone kit by itself. The Fokker Eindecker is plane with quite simple shapes and colours, making the engine a big focal point of the whole model. I painted the Oberursel U.I engine quite simply by spraying it with Aluminium Alclad II. The motor itself is really rich in details, so there really is no need for any special painting effects. Weathering of engine was really simple, an oil wash with dark brown-grey colours was absolutely sufficient to create contrast between all those tiny cylinder ribs.

To mount an engine like this which is quite exact in scale size, you will also need also a scale thickness aftermarket cowling piece. Fortunately Aviattic have already prepared one, It is thin as paper and in combination with its photoetched parts it will provide the perfect cover for my rotary engine.

The wings of the Fokker E.III in 1:32 scale are quite a large areas and we can't just leave them painted in one solid colour. In this scale, they need some colour variation to look realistic. After painting them with the base field grey colour, I sprayed thin highlight with a lightened shade around the ribs.

After everything was painted and all the parts assembled, I was approaching the grand finale, weathering! The first step was once again done using filters. These were created the same way as in interior with thinned enamel colours. I used light dusty and dark brown and grey colours. Filters will give a nice dusty look to all the surfaces. Application is easy, just soak a brush in the filter, remove excess so it will just moisten the surface, not flood it and apply it over all areas.

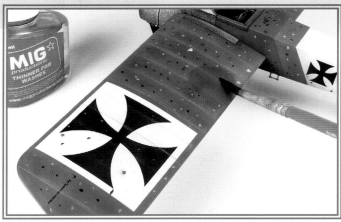

The second step of the final weathering is the classic technique that can't be omitted - the wash. I used brown, grey and black oil colours mix thinned with thinners and applied with a thin brush around all details and recesses. There are not many on the surface of Fokker E.III, so you can do this step quite quickly.

Fading will enhance desired colour variations even more. It is also quite simple to achieve, Apply assorted oil colors directly from tubes in small dots over the model and then blend them with a wet brush onto the surface.

Dusty parts of undercarriage and tail can be replicated by overspraying these areas with diluted Tamia Buff and Flat Earth colours.

And then enhanced by applying dry dust and earth colour pigments with a soft brush.

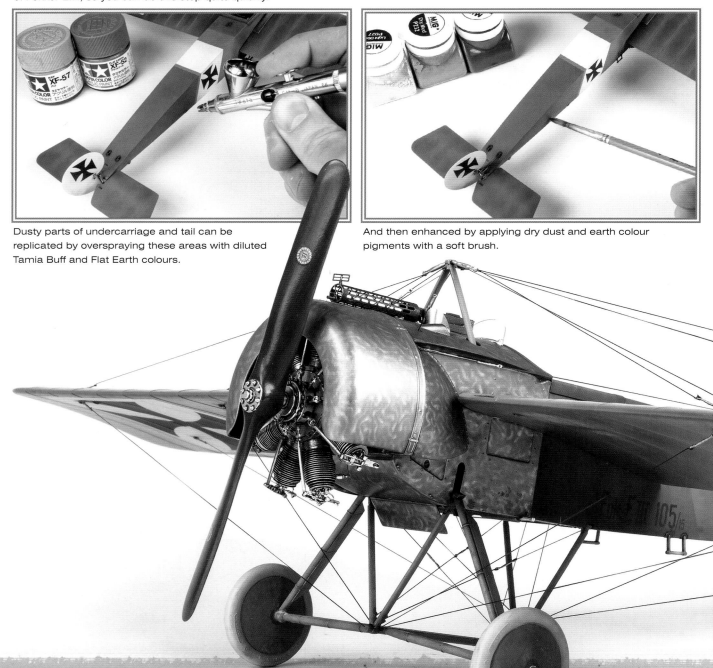

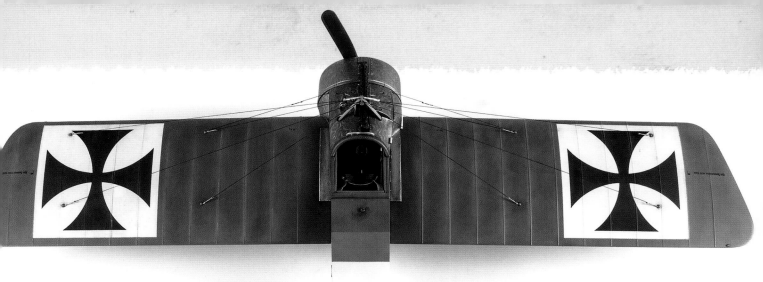

After mandatory rigging, which consists of only a few simple lines this time and can be easily done with elastic EZ line glued with superglue, we are finished with this attractive and simple model.

FINE
100 Feet
30.5 Meters
E Z Line
Stretch that lasts

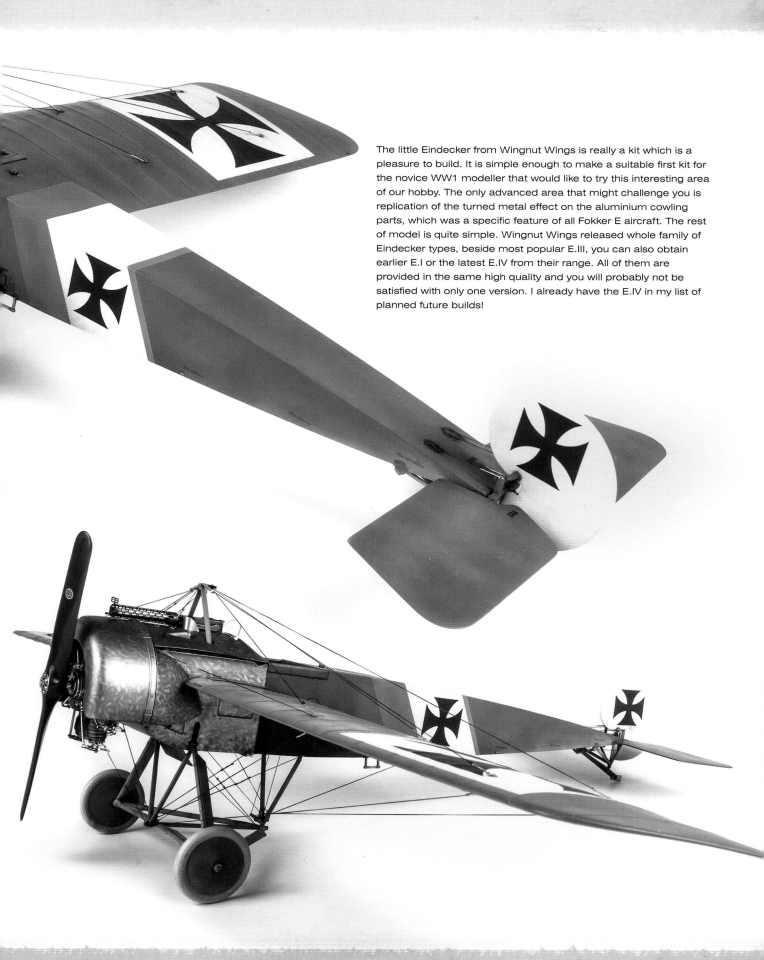

The little Eindecker from Wingnut Wings is really a kit which is a pleasure to build. It is simple enough to make a suitable first kit for the novice WW1 modeller that would like to try this interesting area of our hobby. The only advanced area that might challenge you is replication of the turned metal effect on the aluminium cowling parts, which was a specific feature of all Fokker E aircraft. The rest of model is quite simple. Wingnut Wings released whole family of Eindecker types, beside most popular E.III, you can also obtain earlier E.I or the latest E.IV from their range. All of them are provided in the same high quality and you will probably not be satisfied with only one version. I already have the E.IV in my list of planned future builds!

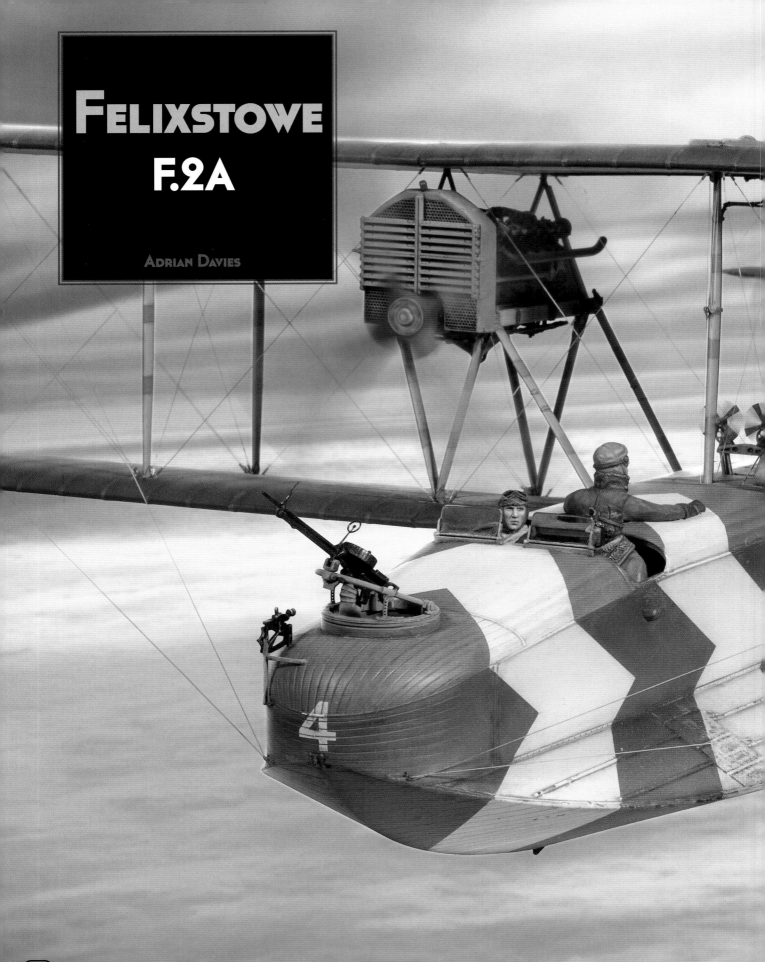

FELIXSTOWE
F.2A

ADRIAN DAVIES

IF I HAD TO DEFINE MYSELF AS A MODEL MAKER IT WOULD BE PRIMARILY AS A BUILDER IN 1/72ND SCALE OF WORLD WAR II MULTI ENGINED AIRCRAFT. I ALSO HAVE AN INTEREST IN SOME OF THEIR PREDECESSORS, AIRCRAFT SUCH AS THE FELIXSTOWE.

Over the years I've collected a little of the available reference on these colourful flying boats, with the intention of building a 1/72nd scale model using the Roden kit as a basis. Then in October 2014, Wingnut Wings announced release of not one, but three separate kits of the Felixstowe. I do not normally work in 1/32nd scale, but given Wingnut Wings's formidable (and justified) reputation for quality, I figured that if I was going to build a model of this aircraft, I may as well go large.

A sentence from J.M. Bruce's Windsock Datafile on the Felixstowe has always stuck with me: "Our greatest foes are not the enemy, but our own petrol pipes." So ended Captain R. Leckie's report after a dogfight that involved five Felixstowes and various Hansa Brandenburg float planes. Leckie's comment refers to two of the Felixstowes being hampered not by German action but the fragile nature of the aircraft's fuel system, a system that on occasion required the engineer to climb out on to the wing to affect repairs, sometimes in flight.

Now there is an idea for a model!

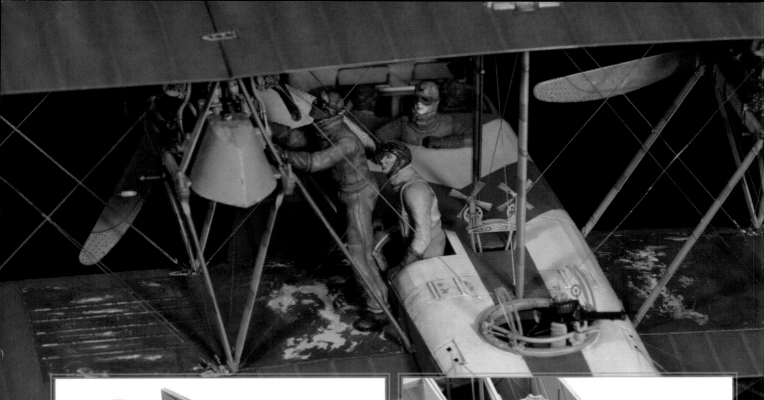

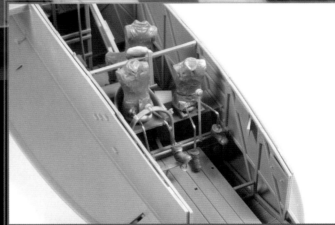

The Figures

I am no figure sculptor or painter. My only experience of figure modelling was painting two commercial figures for an aircraft vignette. I am a great admirer of this aspect of our hobby, so much so that I collect a lot of books that describe the techniques used by figure modellers, thinking that maybe one day I would take the plunge. The book that gave me the push to finally have a go was Made in Holland published by AFV Modeller, specifically Luc Klinker's chapter describing a half track full of figures of his own creation.

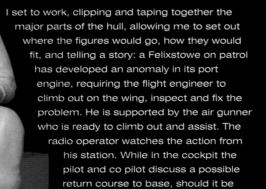

I set to work, clipping and taping together the major parts of the hull, allowing me to set out where the figures would go, how they would fit, and telling a story: a Felixstowe on patrol has developed an anomaly in its port engine, requiring the flight engineer to climb out on the wing, inspect and fix the problem. He is supported by the air gunner who is ready to climb out and assist. The radio operator watches the action from his station. While in the cockpit the pilot and co pilot discuss a possible return course to base, should it be needed.

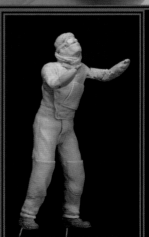

Once I had the basic narrative established, it was time to let loose with Apoxie Sculpt, some Hornet heads, wire and some parts from a Tamiya British Infantry set. I started with the pilot, then as he progressed I moved on to the next crew member. When all five crew men were done It became apparent that the first (the pilot) was not up to the standard of the last one, so a re-sculpt was in order. I must admit that as crude as these are by other modellers' standards, I greatly enjoyed doing them and look forward to getting better at them.

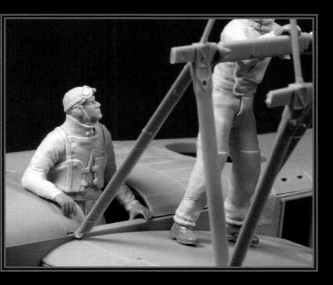

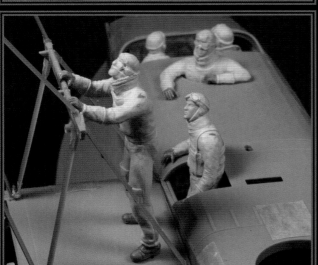

The figures were painted using Vallejo acrylics. I took care to vary the colours of the crewmen's Sidcot Suits to break up the monochrome of four figures dressed the same. I know that anyone standing in the slipstream of an aircraft would be wearing face and eye protection but I took a little artistic license here.

INTERIOR

Back to the familiar territory of being an aircraft model maker. The interior is completely out of the box with just a couple of mooring ropes added, the one in the bow conveniently hiding the internal seam in the outer hull.

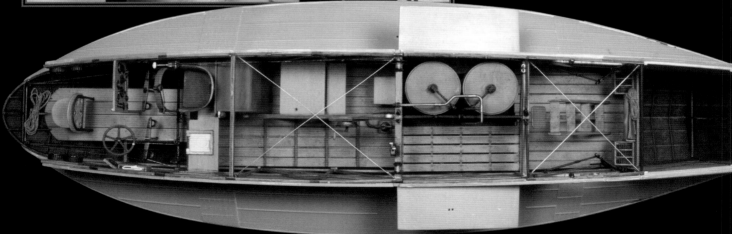

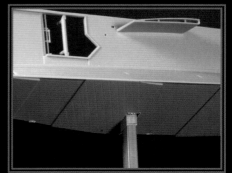

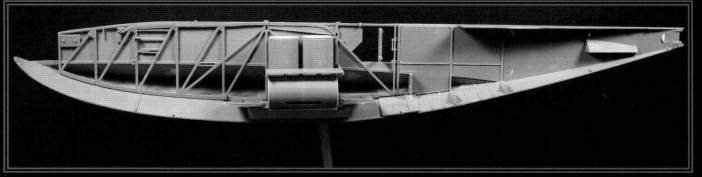

It took a little thought to work out how to support such a large model "in flight". The large internal fuel tanks provided a convenient place to embed a piece of square section Albion Alloy tubing, and into this tube it would be easy to slip another telescoping square tube that would form the stand itself. Packing the void in the fuel tank with Apoxie Sculpt, coupled with Wingnut Wings's strong engineering, gave a remarkably solid connection for supporting a model of this size.

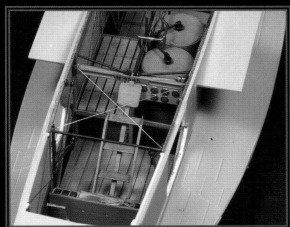

Painting followed, and was (at least to me) a challenge, taking three separate attempts to get right. The wood grain was simulated using thinned oil paints over a base of Tamiya paint, showing three wood types: the mahogany of the main frame, the sheet material (marine plywood?) of the sides and the dimensional timber used on less important parts such as the floor boards. I realise that a great deal of this would be lost when the hull was closed, but a kit of this quality just screamed out to be painted.

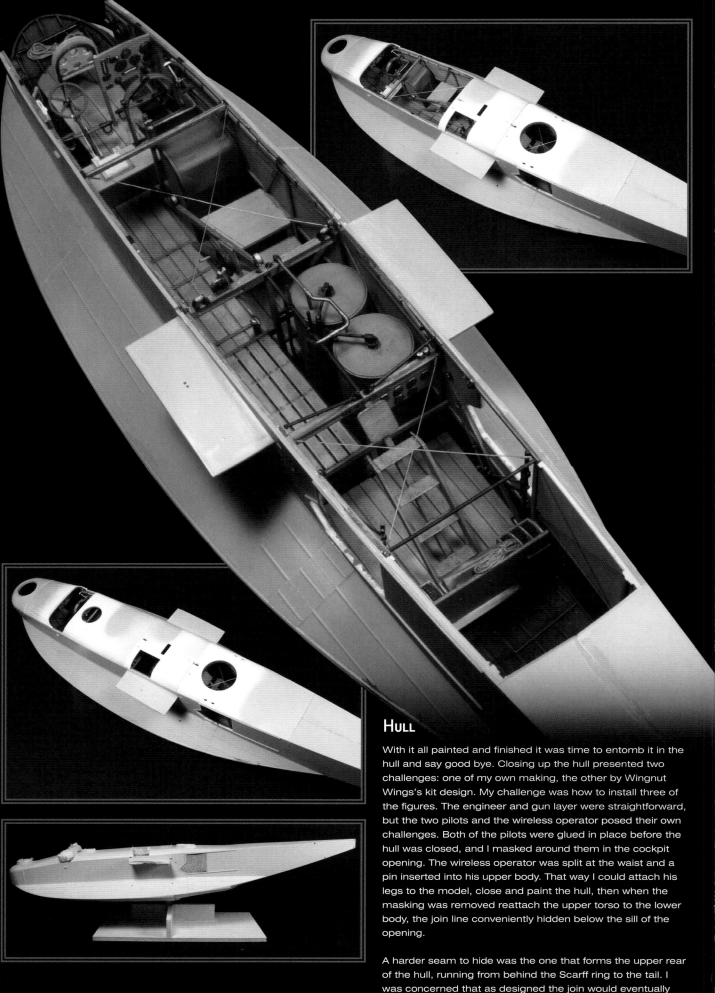

HULL

With it all painted and finished it was time to entomb it in the hull and say good bye. Closing up the hull presented two challenges: one of my own making, the other by Wingnut Wings's kit design. My challenge was how to install three of the figures. The engineer and gun layer were straightforward, but the two pilots and the wireless operator posed their own challenges. Both of the pilots were glued in place before the hull was closed, and I masked around them in the cockpit opening. The wireless operator was split at the waist and a pin inserted into his upper body. That way I could attach his legs to the model, close and paint the hull, then when the masking was removed reattach the upper torso to the lower body, the join line conveniently hidden below the sill of the opening.

A harder seam to hide was the one that forms the upper rear of the hull, running from behind the Scarff ring to the tail. I was concerned that as designed the join would eventually

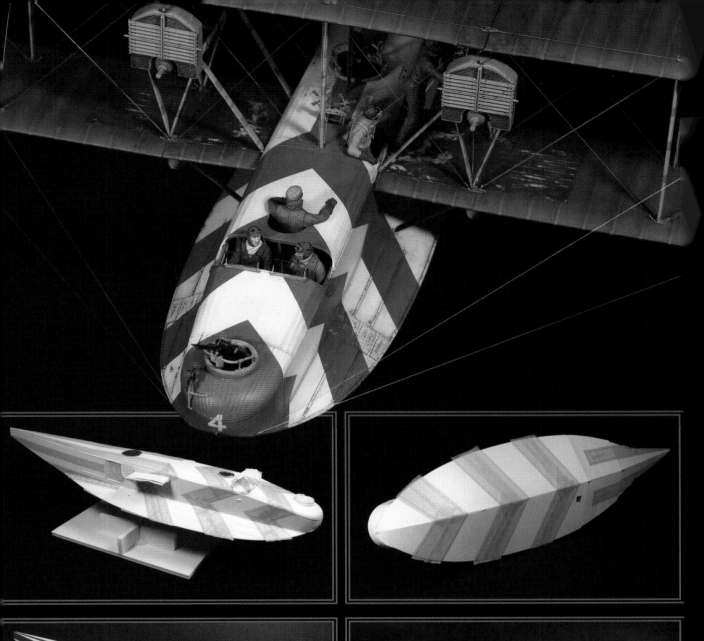

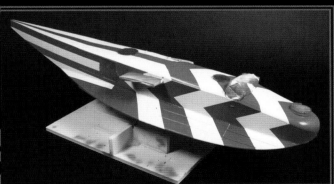

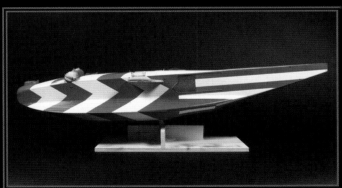

split leaving a seam that would be hard to repair. Especially with my intent of showing the aircraft in flight and the different forces acting on that joint from if it was displayed in its beaching trolley as the designers intended. After the hull was glued together, a plate of 0.75mm styrene was glued to the top of the hull, covering everything from the rear of the Scarff ring to the leading edge of the tail. When this had hardened, it was then sanded to blend it carefully in with the rest of the airframe. Resulting in the complete covering of any awkward seams, and the confidence that no matter what, it will never "pop" or show as a seam.

EXTERIOR AND PAINT

popular subject for model makers, colour schemes. I've read a lot of articles that describe them as "dazzle" patterns. Whilst they are dazzling, that was not the intent. In the dogfight described in the report, the flight of five Felixstowes (most in the same PC10 and natural wood finish) lost unit cohesion, with confusion as to who was the flight leader and whom to follow. As a result, the naval flights at Felixstowe and Great Yarmouth repainted each aircraft in its own unique scheme, using the stocks of paint available at the time. So rather than to confuse an enemy pilot, the scheme was to clarify the situation for the RNAS/RAF pilot. Its other advantage was that it would be easier to spot an aircraft should it come down in the open seas.

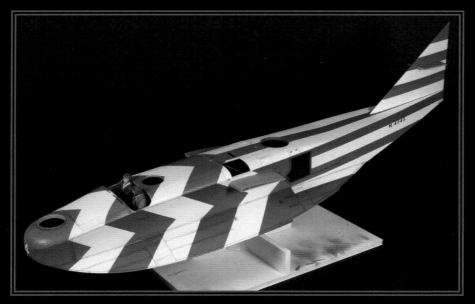

With all the openings masked and the hull mounted on a stand, painting could begin. A favourite white paint of mine is Tamiya's fine white primer in a spray can. Light coats of this were sprayed on, straight out of the can, with the spray can sitting in a bath of warm water, to warm the paint. I find this gave a lovely satin white finish that was both bright and tough. After leaving the model for a week for the paint to harden, it was time to start the stripes. On a photocopier I enlarged to 1/32nd scale a copy of the Ronny Bar's artwork. Bar's artwork is based on the same 3D model that Wingnut Wings developed of the aircraft, so the outlines are completely in sync with the kit. Using measurements from the artwork, I carefully plotted points onto the model, then masking could commence. I knew that the alignment and quality of the stripes would make or break the project, so after taking a day off work and, for 8 hours very carefully applying 2 1/2 rolls of Nichiban tape, I reached a point where I was comfortable airbrushing the red.

For the red, I used Tamiya's gloss red acrylic thinned with Tamiya thinners. Adam Wilder's work, which I had seen in a friend's collection, inspired me to try my hand at modulation. The shape of the Felixstowe's hull lends itself to this technique. Peeling back the tape was a lot of fun. The red was extremely vibrant, this

is exactly what I wanted. Better that than it look dull from the outset.

With the paint on the hull dry, I applied filters of Paynes Grey oil paint, to homogenise the colours, while still allowing some of the vibrancy to show through. Being mindful of what material was under which part of the hull (was it plywood, mahogany or pitch?), I completed pin washing, weathering and chipping of the hull.

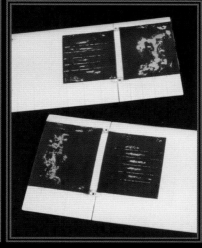

The Wings

The wings, at a little over a meter long, provided their own challenge. I was keen to use Aviattic's decal sheets to replicate not only the Clear Doped Linen (CDL) but also the PC10 doped upper surfaces. Starting with the wings themselves, they were all cleaned up, and assembled, then painted in Tamiya's fine surface primer. When this had hardened I added a generous coat of Gunze Clear Coat, again straight out of the spray-can. This gave me an extremely tough high gloss finish. Before starting on the decals, I set to painting the plywood decks on either side of the engine mounts. These were painted a wood tone, followed by a coat of hairspray and a top coat of Tamiya acrylic. I chipped the paint using a wet brush. Some further weathering followed.

At first the decals were more than a little daunting. With over 430 individual decals it took some time. Rather than risk applying a single decal to each wing surface, I decided to break the decals into smaller sections using the wing ribs as a guide. I could hide any joints with rib tape decals applied later. Using the RFC CDL printed on clear decal, I started with the underside, first applying every other decal, then the next evening filling in the gaps. A word of caution about the decals, their colour and tone is not consistent across the sheets, so it is important to keep track from which sheet and where you cut the decal to maintain a consistent finish. Otherwise the wing will start to look patchy. After applying the base layer of CDL and a coat of Future,

it was time for the individual rib tapes. For these I used the RFC CDL sheet, but this time printed on white decal film, giving me the simulation of Clear Doped Linen I hoped for. Another coat of Future and it's time to turn over the wing.

The upper surface PC10 was done in very much the same way. I used Aviattic's PC10 printed on clear decal for the fabric, and PC10 printed on white decal for the rib tapes. I made some small templates from thick vellum to help with cutting around fittings and details. I also made sure that the decals were cut long enough to wrap around the leading edge of the wing rather than try and butt join them. Another coat of Future sealed the final decals and then I

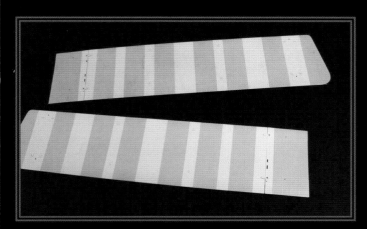

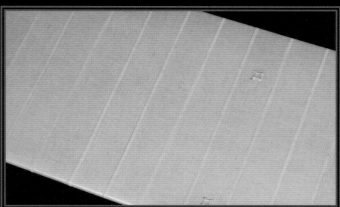

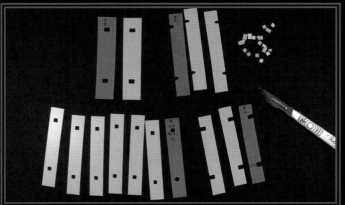

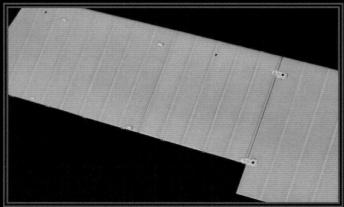

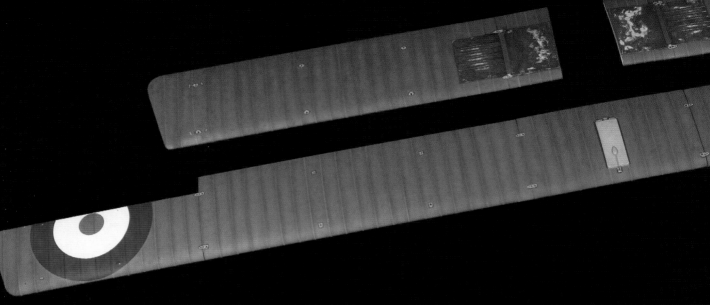

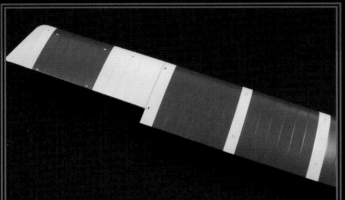

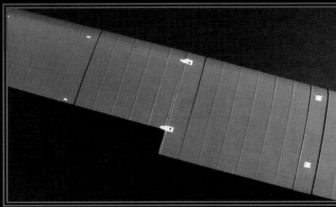

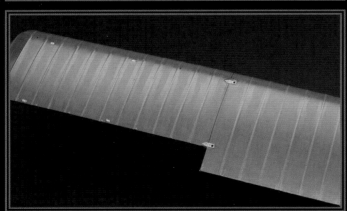

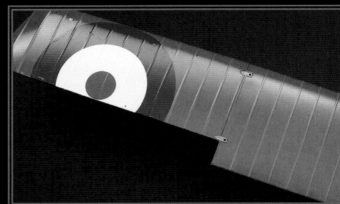

applied the kit supplied cockades. Yet another coat of Future and a coat of flat. I used Vallejo for the final touch-up and detail painting. To break the flatness of the finish without obscuring the linen texture in the decals, I very thinly applied a few airbrushed filters of Tamiya paint. Finished with some fuel, oil and dirt applications using various AK Interactive products the wings were put aside till needed.

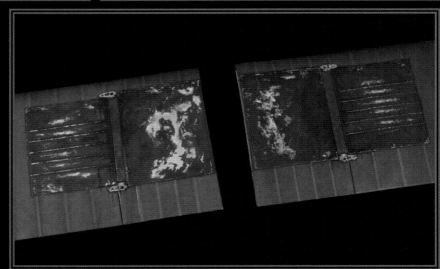

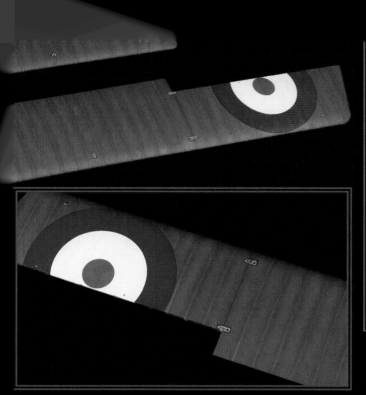

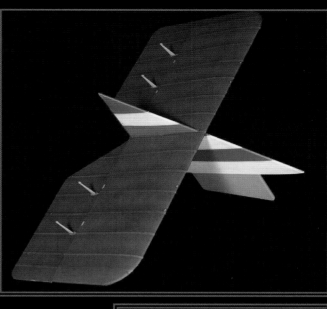

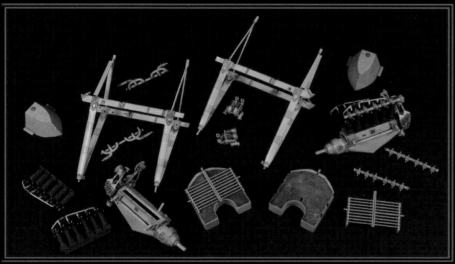

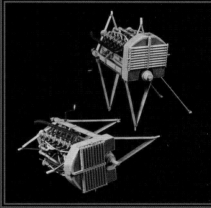

Engines and Details

After the many evenings spent covering and finishing the wings, the engines and other details were a treat. I made no additions to the engines, just careful assembly and painting. I added a bungee cord to the Scarff ring, made with some fine solder. I made replacement thrust plates for the front of the two propellers using the bolts carefully shaved from the existing kit parts, glued to new plates cut from vellum. Separating the plates from the propeller greatly eased painting, giving a much crisper finish. If there is anything I would suggest to the good people at Wingnut Wings, it would be to engineer the propellers with separate plates. After all, they usually are at the very front of the model.

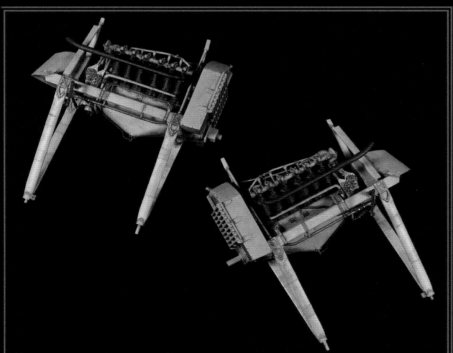

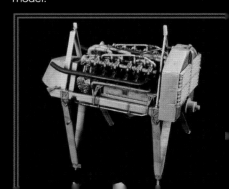

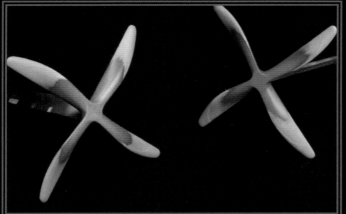
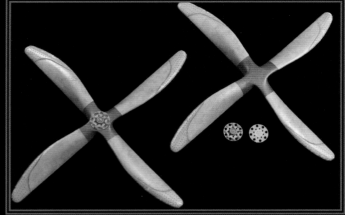

Wingnut Wings are extremely clever with the design of the struts. Despite all looking the same, they only fit one way, and so with careful examination it is impossible to install them in the wrong order. I devised a jig to mount all the struts in order and keep them in position relative to each other. This in turn allowed me to paint all the struts without making a mess, and line up the light grey decal film used to represent the linen cord bindings that feature so prominently on the aircraft I was building.

FINAL ASSEMBLY AND RIGGING

A model of this size needs a steady base on which to be assembled. Using the kit provided beaching trolley as a basis, I constructed a jig on which to assemble the aircraft, ensuring that it was square and aligned. Before the upper wing was placed on the model, I systematically drilled holes for and glued in anchors from Bob's Buckles. Then I put in all the rigging lines to the underside of the top wing. For the lines I used two thicknesses of Rio Flouroflex tippet line (3x and 5x) which gave me the desired difference in thickness as specified by the Wingnut Wings instructions. To simulate turnbuckles I used 2mm lengths of polyamide tubing sealed with cyanoacrylate glue.

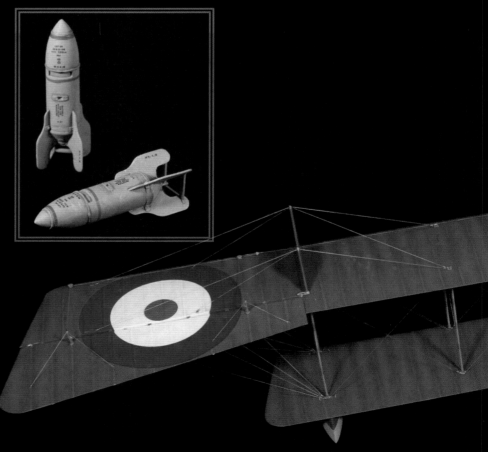

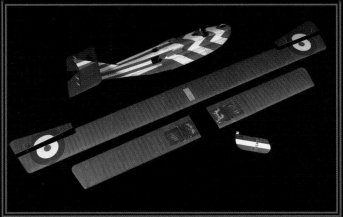

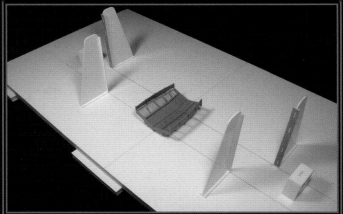

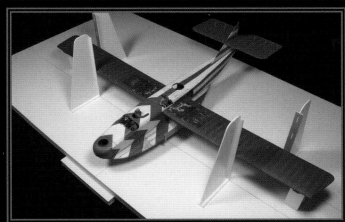

With many struts to feed into their respective holes, placing the top wing was a challenge. The jig was a great help. Soon it was time to start tying the upper wing to the lower, working methodically from the centre outwards. The rigging helped the wings achieve a lot of rigidity, thankfully as the wings would have no other support. I was reminded of an essay by the USAF historian Richard Hallion, where he posited that one of the greatest advances in aeronautical engineering was the Pratt truss, invented in 1844. It gave engineers a system for making lightweight yet extremely rigid structures. The wings of a biplane being a perfect example and working today holding the wings of my Felixstowe in perfect order.

With the last rigging line tightened, it was time to move on to the control lines and some of the outer rigging. I was concerned that the tension in the rigging would cause the wing tips and control horns to deform. So instead of the Tippet line, I used EZ line, giving the lines a constant tension without putting stress on the control surfaces or wingtips. When done, I painted the lines with Alclad Duraluminium applied with a fine brush.

The moment of truth. The jig disassembled, the aircraft was ready to be mounted on its stand. After a session of attaching detail parts, touch ups and last bits of weathering, she was done.

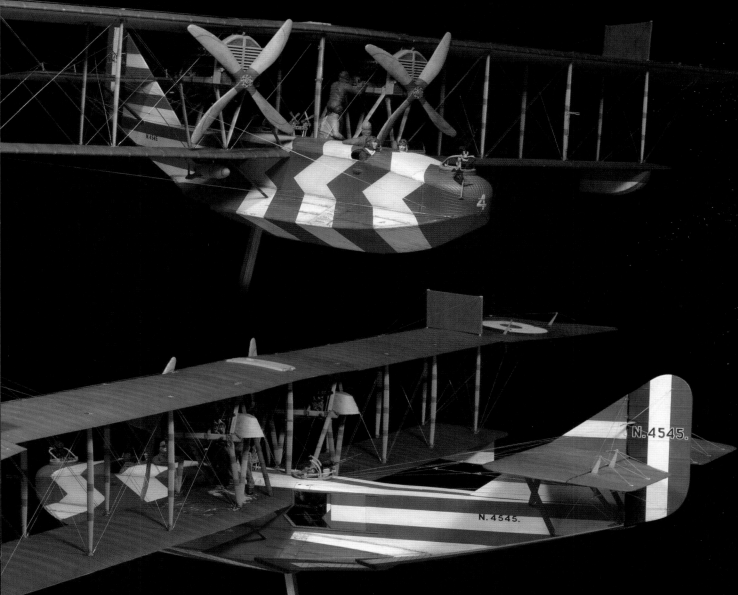

Conclusion

This is the second Wingnut Wings that I have completed, the first was their FE2b. They are lovely kits to build, producing startling results using some very clever engineering. My only advice to anyone considering building one of these, is that as well-designed as they are, they will punish sloppy building habits. Anyone who is careful in the build will be greatly rewarded, but if care is neglected you will have less than a great experience.

It took a little over two and a half years to finish this model. I am forever grateful to my fellow members of IPMS Vagabonds, and my friends Dario Giuliano and Marian Holly for their constant encouragement and insight. I would like to dedicate this build to Roger Razor, an early supporter of the project, who unfortunately isn't here to see it finished. Blue skies.

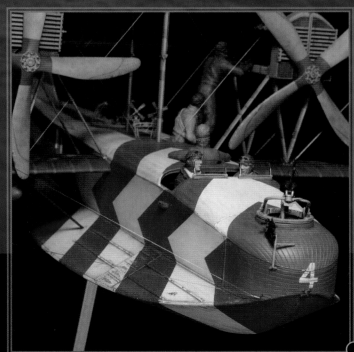

SOPWITH SNIPE

MICHEL GRUSON

FOLLOWING THE SOPWITH PUP AND THE TRIPLANE, WINGNUT WINGS REWARDS US WITH A BEAUTIFUL REPRODUCTION OF THE LAST FIGHTER PLANE MANUFACTURED BY SOPWITH; THE LATE VERSION OF THE SNIPE.
AS IN THE PAST, WINGNUTS HAVE BROUGHT TOGETHER ALL THE NECESSARY INGREDIENTS TO CREATE A SUPERB REPRODUCTION OF THIS 1:32 MODEL.

The model is conceived in a simple way which will please many an airplane model enthusiast. Among the 5 possible markings, I chose the one from the plane captured by the Russians in 1920, with sober but original markings with an ace of spades on the sides of the aircraft, "Nelly" written on the right side and black stars on the wings, such as the ones from Wingnut Wings.

The assembly begins with painting the interior of the fuselage but only after having previously defined what the different parts are made of: wood, plywood, fabric and metal. We begin by painting the metallic part at the front of the fuselage. Then the parts that are covered with fabric are painted in Tamiya XF55, whilst the mountings and reinforcements of the footholds on the left side are painted brown.

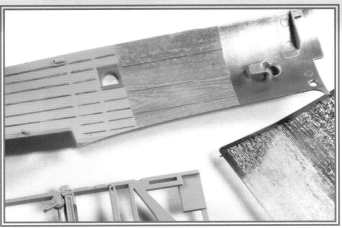

All the pieces and zones made of "wood" are first given a coat of clear acrylic (Gunze H315). The plywood, where the cockpit is, is also given a base coat of (Gunze H79) paint using the photo etched stencil from Radu Brinzan. Using it is quite simple and allows you to create an imitation plywood effect. The "wood" is finished off using a coat of oil paints; yellow ochre and burnt umber.
They are applied using a paint brush to simulate the wood's natural grain. Three days are needed for the paint to dry before being handling.

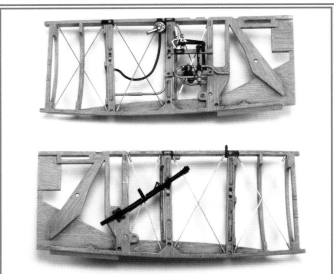

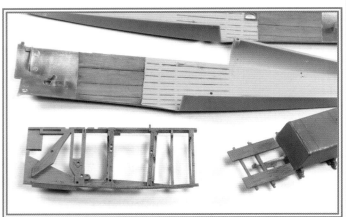

The ammunition magazine of the machine guns, as well as the two fluid tanks, is painted with XF 82 grey and then abundantly weathered with acrylic inks and pigments.

The cockpit is particularly complete and accurate, which makes the assembly and painting most pleasant. Nonetheless, a few modifications are made, such as the control cables and the internal stiffeners made out of different materials (stretched plastic and photoetched parts).

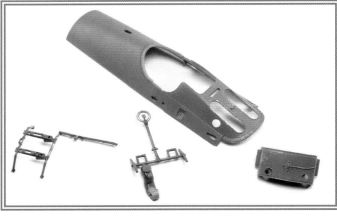

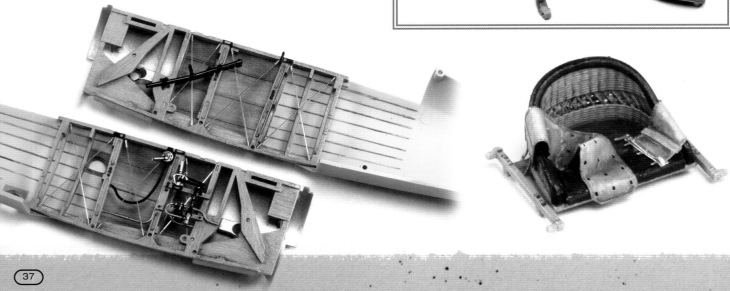

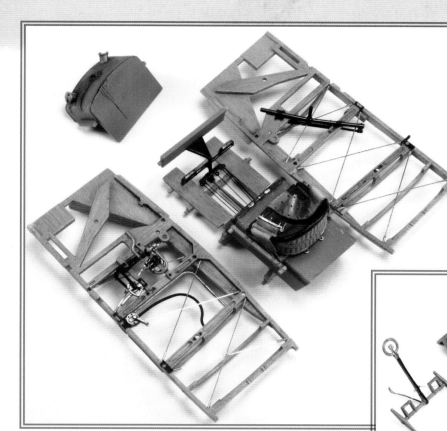

The pilot's seat, made partly of wicker, is reproduced very well. It is painted in the same way as the parts made of wood but with a slightly lighter shade. The leather cushion and padding are painted with prince August acrylic paint before being lightly dry-brushed with a light shade of yellow. The photo-etched safety harnesses are painted with different beige and brown tones of acrylic paints that are blended to create a realistic transition from one shade to the next.

The consoles, joysticks and other details are painted with several shades of Prince August acrylics.
Once painted, the dial decals are applied to the instrument panel. To give the impression of glass, a drop of white glue is put into each dial.

The guns are fine representations and the photo etched sets provide more precision. Generally they are painted black and are dry brushed with aluminium. On the photo etched loading handle, a small ball of white glue is formed to reproduce the wooden pommel.

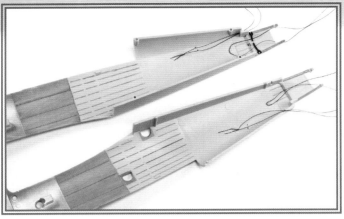

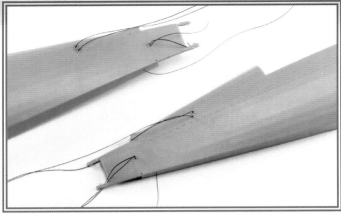

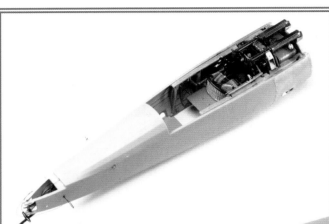

Before closing the fuselage, EZ line is glued to the interior of the fuselage halves for the elevator rigging. When the time comes, all you have to do is to pull on the cables to attach them to the elevator control horns.

The assembly of the cockpit is completed with no difficulties whatsoever, all the pieces fit into place easily; this brings us to joining the two fuselage halves, which, if this stage has been well prepared beforehand, won't need any putty.

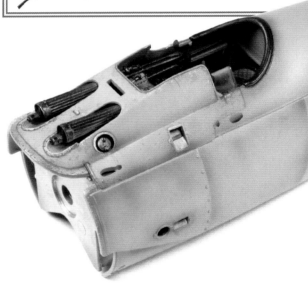

There are very few parts to this rotary Bentley engine, however the details are extremely well reproduced and what's more the instructions, that are clear with many photos, will enable us to carry out the assembly without difficulty. This won't prevent a slight improvement to the details by adding spark plug wires that need to be carefully pulled taut.

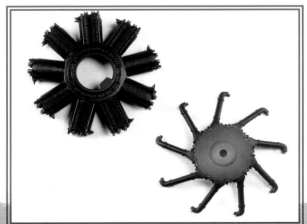

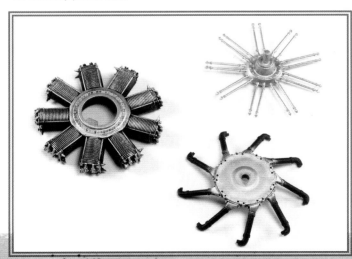

All the pieces are painted before being assembled; the cylinders with a combination of black and brown, then dry brushed with Rub n Buff, the pipes are painted red/brown, the engine block and the pushrods are only given a coat of aluminium paint. Concerning the weathering, it is achieved using acrylic ink and pigments diluted with water. The pipes are given special treatment with a coat of blue, rust and black Tamiya pigments that are applied so that they create a gradual transition in colour.

The engine cowls, after being painted with Rub 'n Buff, are weathered before being fixed into place. To do this, randomly spray with very diluted brown and black paint to create tonal gradation. Finally, staining from fluids is simulated with sepia ink.

The part near to the propeller is painted a "wood" colour before painting the extremities: the front of the blades in grey XF82 and the back green/black. Then it is weathered using Tamiya pigments mixed with water and applied with a brush.

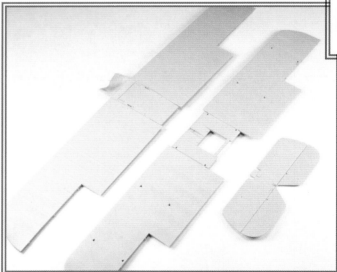

Painting and weathering:

We start with the underside using Tamiya XF 55 paint that is generously sprayed all over. Having decided to highlight the reinforcements of the fabric and the structure, several layers of a slightly darker shade are sprayed as close to the reinforcements as possible taking care to mask them using Post-its for example.
As you can see on the photo, I first of all began to the left of the grooves. You need to work from the left side to the right so as not to put the stencil on the freshly painted parts. Once finished on one side, all that needs to be done is to paint the other side working

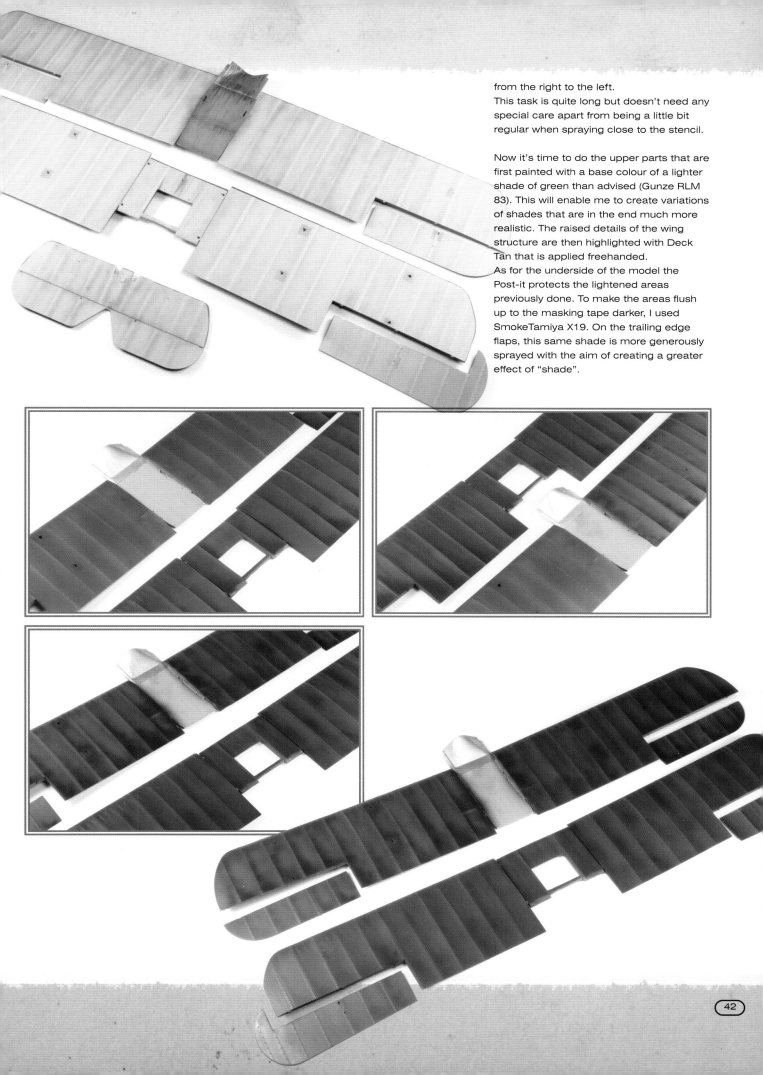

from the right to the left.
This task is quite long but doesn't need any special care apart from being a little bit regular when spraying close to the stencil.

Now it's time to do the upper parts that are first painted with a base colour of a lighter shade of green than advised (Gunze RLM 83). This will enable me to create variations of shades that are in the end much more realistic. The raised details of the wing structure are then highlighted with Deck Tan that is applied freehanded.
As for the underside of the model the Post-it protects the lightened areas previously done. To make the areas flush up to the masking tape darker, I used SmokeTamiya X19. On the trailing edge flaps, this same shade is more generously sprayed with the aim of creating a greater effect of "shade".

On the fuselage the same thing is done to highlight the wooden structure under the fabric. Deck tan is sprayed above the raised details whereas X19 SmokeTamiya is sprayed on the lower parts. The aim is to create effects of light and shading to give added depth.

Finally black/green XF70 Tamiya is sprayed to blend and minimize the exaggerated contrast on the areas previously painted.

The difficulty is to dose the paint so that the contrasts are minimized without making them disappear altogether. Basically, you have to stop before totally destroying your painstaking work.

For the markings, I chose not to use the decals provided by Wingnut Wings. I'm going to use other stencils as the markings and roundels are easier to do. This choice will enable me to create nuances with the different shades more easily.

Let's begin with the stars on the wings that are first painted Gunze Tire black. Then the reinforcements are highlighted, again using a Post-it; I masked the reinforcements before spraying black paint flush to the edge of it. The same thing is done for the "Ace of Spades" on the fuselage.

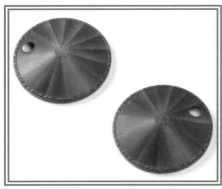

The wheels are superb representations as you can clearly see the spokes under the fabric. They are also painted in the same way to create light and shadow effects. But beforehand the inside of the flanges are painted with Clear Doped Linen and metal spokes are added so that they are visible through the access hole to the valve. The legs are painted black and the bungee suspension cords, that are accurately represented, are painted light beige. The whole thing is then heavily weathered with Tamiya pigments. Note that this assembly fits perfectly to the fuselage and the wings.

It's now time to move on to the weathering stage to make our model more realistic. To do this the effects of light and shadow are going to be highlighted.
I chose to do this mainly with oil paints using three colours: Naples yellow, burnt umber and black. Without being diluted, they are applied using a paint brush and are spread out as much as possible. Oil paints are perfect for this job for they take longer to dry, so you can mix them and determine the degree of opacity of the shade by taking off the paint, if necessary, with a cotton bud, or even wiping it off with white spirit.

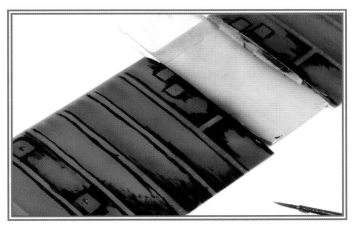

We begin by applying black paint on the areas that are hidden from the light, after of course having determined from which direction you want the source of light to come from.
Naples yellow is then applied to all the prominent and "bulging" parts with the aim of creating volume. Brown is used on the in-between areas to blend the colours and create more contrast. This job is quite long but in the end makes the model more realistic.

We finish the weathering using earth-coloured Tamiya pigments to "dirty" the areas where the crew would have walked on the lower area. Spatterings of mud are created by "tapping" a piece of sponge dipped in pigment thinned with water around the undercarriage, along the lower part of the fuselage and at the base of the tailplane.

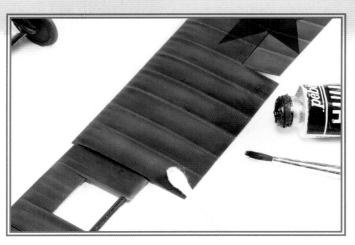

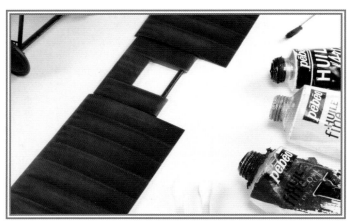

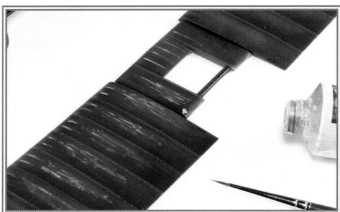

Finally a few fluid streaks are added around the filler caps and around the cowls using acrylic sepia ink.
All that needs to be done now is to seal everything up with a coat of matt varnish.

The interplane and cabane struts are painted XF 82, their metal bracket is painted black, where they meet black and grey shades are applied and Smoke Tamiya is sprayed to darken this area. They are then weathered and made to look used with Tamiya pigments that are diluted with water. These parts are fixed to the fuselage and wings without any problems.

The very precise instructions will make the task easier as several drawings show the difference between the control cables (green) and the aerodynamic wires (blue). Concerning the flat RAF aerodynamic wires, I used the photo etch set from Radu Brizan Production.
They are a joy to work with as they are rigid and are easy to use. First of all they need to be cut to the right length. Then small sections of Model FactoyHiro flexible microtube are inserted into each extremity. Make sure the rigging is slightly longer so that they can be inserted into the eyelets provided.

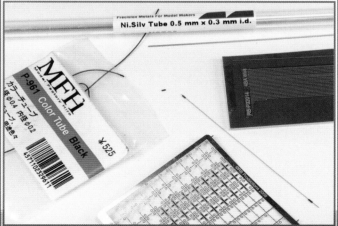

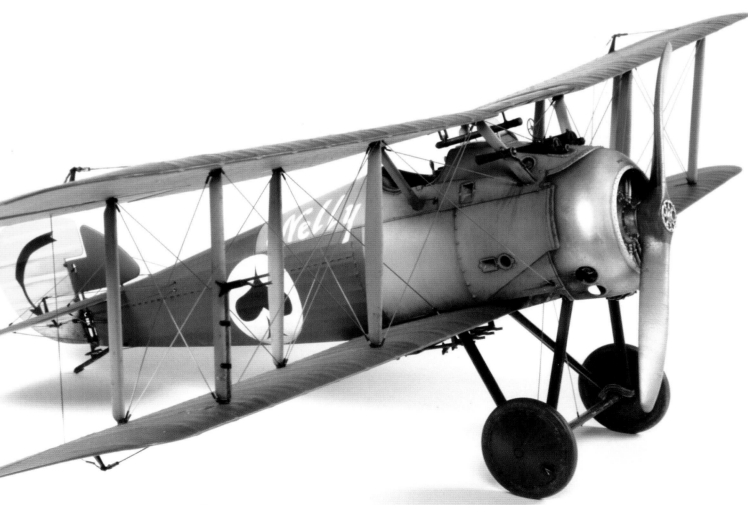

RUMPLER
C.IV EARLY

RICHARD CAMION

I HAVE TO ADMIT THAT I WAS FAIRLY
EXCITED BUILD THE RUMPLER ALTHOUGH IT
WAS NOT AN AIRCRAFT THAT I KNEW VERY
MUCH ABOUT. THE ATTRACTIVE BOXART FOR
THE WINGNUT WINGS KIT SHOWS OFF THE
THE FLOWING FISH-SHAPED FUSELAGE,
BUILT FOR SPEED. TO ENHANCE MY
KNOWLEDGE AND TO HELP WITH THE
PROJECT I ALSO PURCHASED A COPY OF
WINDSOCK DATAFILE No.149 AND HUNTED
AROUND ON THE INTERNET TO SEARCH FOR
ANY IMAGES THAT MIGHT BE HELPFUL.

The Rumpler C.IV was developed to fill the
reconaisance, artillery spotter or light bomber roles,
from the Rumpler C III from which it is directly derived
with some improvements. The engine was upgraded to
the Daimler-Mercedes Benz D.IVa instead of the D.III
and a modified tail. These changes gave the plane an
outstanding performance allowing it to fly higher than
its adversaries. I chose to represent the Rumpler C. IV
6689/16 flown by Alexander Becker in Metz Frescaty in
1917. This two-tone camouflage with flying swan
emblem are very sober and well suited to the lines of
the aircraft.

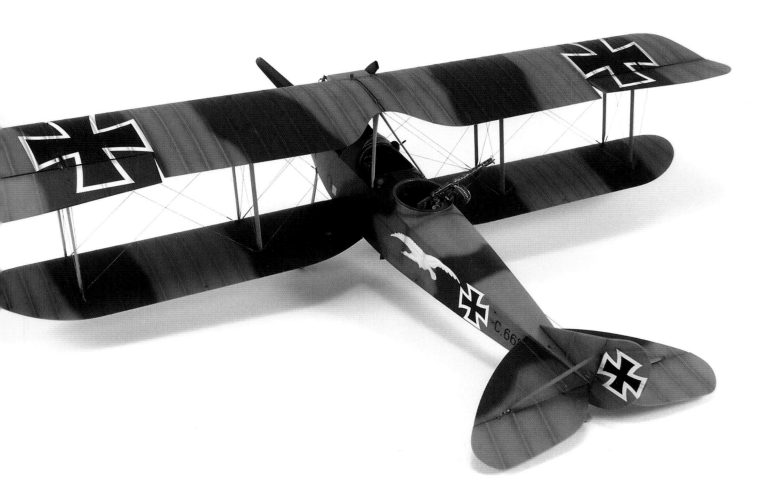

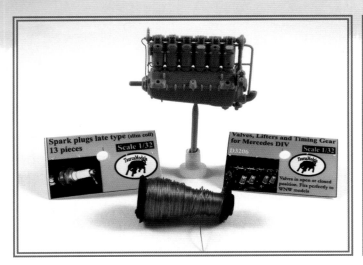

THE DAIMLER-MERCEDES D.IVA ENGINE

The engine is a model within the model, and was assembled according to the instructions. I added additional detail with copper wire and two dedicated resin sets released by Taurus Models to upgrade the spark plugs and valves.

The springs on the valves are set to replicate the ignition cycle of the cylinders so are at different states of compression.

It appears on some archive pictures that the intake manifold was often wrapped with additional heat shielding. I reproduced this by winding fine 0.3 mm copper wire around the part E16 followed by a coating of Mr Surfacer 1000 smoothed with acetone to cover the wire.

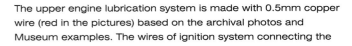

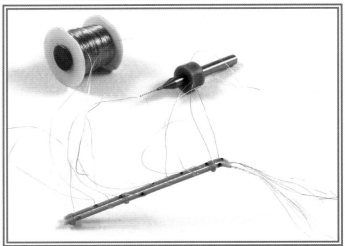

The upper engine lubrication system is made with 0.5mm copper wire (red in the pictures) based on the archival photos and Museum examples. The wires of ignition system connecting the

spark plugs were made of 0.3 mm copper wire and glued to the plug lead tubes in preparation to be connected to the magnetos and spark plugs on each cylinder.

The entire engine was painted matt black. The Sump and Crank Case was drybrushed with a Silver printing ink drybrushed on to reproduce a cast effect on these parts. The top edges of the cylinders, camshafts and valve springs were also drybrushed with the same ink. Lubrication pipes are painted copper and brass parts are painted in using the gold printing ink. The plug leads were painted dark brown. The engine was then suitably weathered using "Oil and Grease Stain Mixture" wash from Mig in several layers.

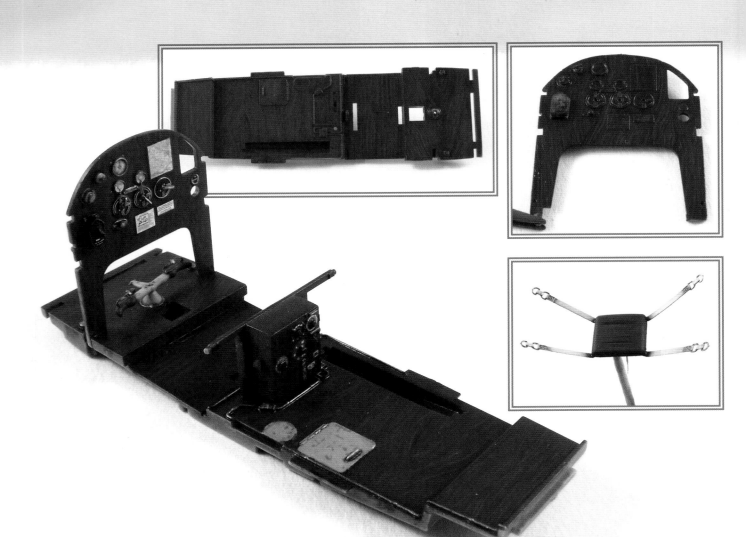

Double Cockpit

Cockpit parts were painted separately before assembly following to the recommended colours from the detailed instructions. I had to select my choice of markings at this point because the choice effects variations in the cockpit arrangement.

Colours

For the wooden parts: a base of Tamiya XF-59 Desert Yellow overlaid with Madder Brown and Crimson Alizarin from Winsor & Newton. After a few minutes of drying (10 to 20), I wiped the oil painted surfaces with an old brush with stiff hairs to simulate wood grain. I used this to vary the the shades of the wooden parts.

The leather seat: Vallejo Gold Brown No. 877 with Burnt Umber oil wash.

Seat harnesses: These are painted using oil paints, a mixture of pale yellow ocher, Naples Yellow and Titanium White. They are shaded with Burnt Umber and highlighted in Titanium White.

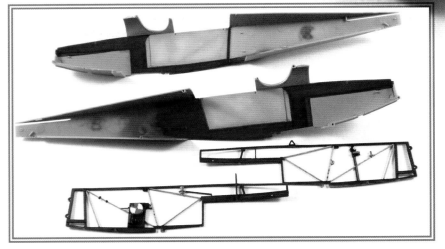

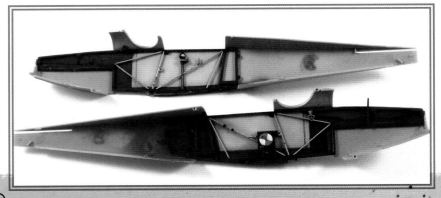

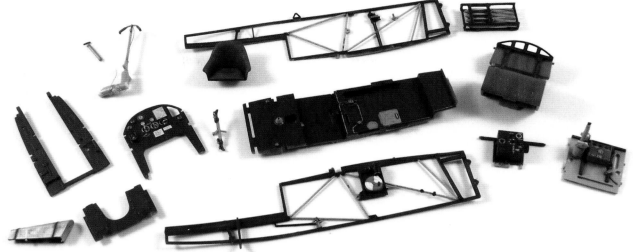

Electrical equipment and fuel tanks: these are painted with Tamiya XF-61 and XF-76. Buttons and dials are brush painted with acrylic paints. Scratches are simulated with touches of silver paint. I painted the bombs and metal struts with Aeromaster RLM 65. The early stick control column is detailed with copper wire simulating the firing control for the machine gun.

BRINGING THE FUSELAGE TOGETHER

With the cockpit, engine and machine gun completed, the cockpit tub was assembled and then inserted into the fuselage. As expected this was problem-free and the tub fitted perfectly into the the fuselage. Careful attention should be payed to the arrangement of the fuselage underside which vary depending on each version, the instructions are really explicit on this point. I was also careful when gluing the tail and the horizontal tailplane so that squareness is perfect, the upper tail struts will be glued later after painting. Particular attention is paid to masking the inside of the fuselage to avoid ruining the work of the interior!

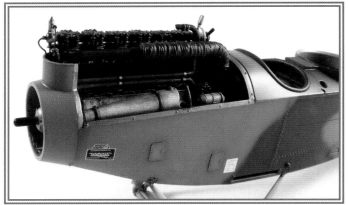

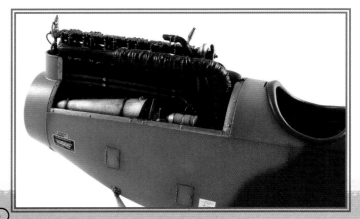

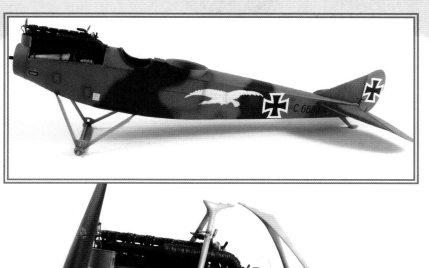

The shades of camouflage I used were Aeromaster RLM65 for the undersides and for the Tamiya XF61 Dark Green and XF-71 Pale Green for the upper surfaces. These colours were nuanced with White XF-2 and Nato black diluted to 90% to shade the stitching and rib details. The decals are placed between two layers of gloss. It took a bit of Micro Sol to soften them especially over the stitching areas. I worked over the markings with the dilute Nato Black to blend them into the finish of the rest of the camouflage. Assorted parts (struts cabin, struts, axle and wheels) are then installed and at the time of assembly, the landing gear rigging and the rudder control cables are installed. They are made of 0.8 mm fishing line and glued in place using CA adhesive.

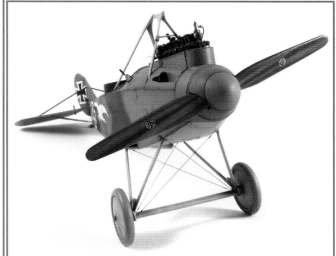

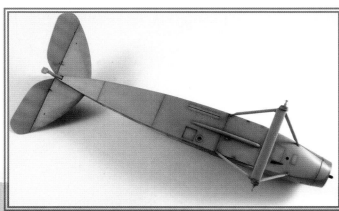

I chose the Axial propeller for this model because I like its shape. I would have prefered the Wolff propellerbut according to the instructions, it was not featured on my chosen aircraft.

A matt white undercoat of Tamiya XF-2 is sprayed to begin with followed by XF-59 "Desert Yellow". I used masking tape and Maskol to hide the base colour to replicate the laminated wooden finis. I used XF-68 "Nato Brown" in two applications: a fine spray pass over the entire propeller and a second full strength pass to pick out certain laminations. Once completely dry the masking was removed and a coat of Mars Brown oil paint was applied over the whole propeller, letting it dry for about ten minutes. With a flat brush brush, I dragged the brush along the propeller lengthwise to simulate the wood grain. Once properly dry the propeller is sprayed with a gloss varnish to apply the "Axial" logo and I finished with a layer of satin varnish.

The wheels are painted in the same way as the lower surfaces using RLM 65. Weathering was applied to suggest the wheel spokes under the covers. The main wheel axle is enhanced with a Burnt Umber and black wash (Oi lpaint and White spirit) defines the seams and the other details of the undercarriage.

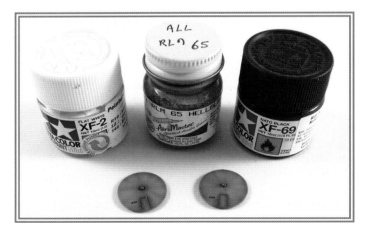

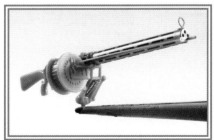

The Observer's Parabellum LMG 14 machine gun is detailed with a replacement barrel sleeve using the replacement barrel set from Master 32024. 0.3mmm copper wire is wrapped around a fine needle to reproduce the springs of the machine gun mount. It was painted in matt black and drybrushed with printing ink.

WINGS

The wings are primed with Warhammer White Skull acrylic paint. The upper surfaces received Tamiya XF-71 first for the pale preen and XF-61 for dark green. The camouflage pattern is quite simple to perform. The base colours were aged with the XF-69 Nato Black. The decals were placed between two coats gloss varnish. The ribs were masked with strips of 0.5mm masking tape and very diluted Nato Black to define the ribs. The edgesof the ribs were drybrushd very gently with Titanium White oil paint.

The pale blue of the lower surfaces is a mixture of Aeromaster RLM-65 and Tamiya XF- 2 Tamiya at approximately an 8:2 ratio. The weathering and shading was done in the same way the same as the upper surfaces.

I use fishing line for the preparation of the rigging. After a thorough study of the rigging scheme in the instructions, I glued each rigging line in place on the upper wing with cyanoacrylate before the wing is installed. At this stage the wing looks incredibly messy with so many wires but in fact it is all quite organsided.

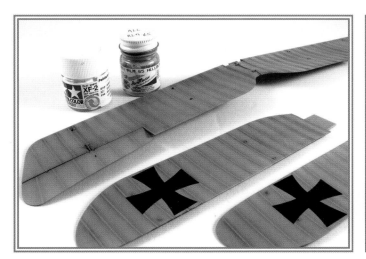

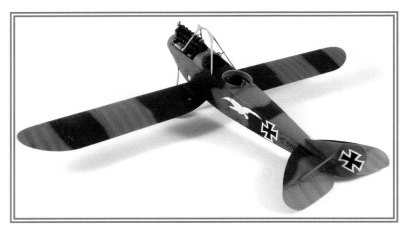

RIGGING THE RUMPLER

To prepare the bracing of the wing rigging lines, I used Bob's Buckles gluing the turnbuckle to each rigging fixing point on the lower wing. They were glued to the fuselage with Mr Hobby Mr Cement S liquid adhesive. The critical moment of biplanes construction is next with the installation of the strutts. Wingnut Wings locator pins certainly make this procedure much easier with positive location points for all the struts. With the upper wing in position I began to tighten the rigging lines, one by one, working from the wing center outwards and alternating between each side to avoid any unwanted distortion. Each line receives a micro tube, the line is passed into the Bob's Buckles ring and returns through the micro tube and is sealed with a drop of cyano glue.

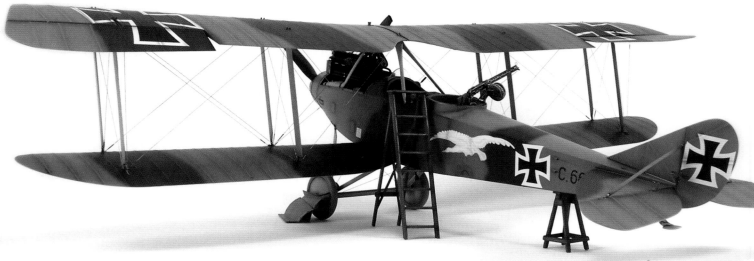

FINAL FLOURISH

To complete the model I also assembled the ladders and tail stand supplied with the kit for a maintenance scenario with the detached engine cowlings. This was another extremely enjoyable project and after all its hard not to be seduced by the look of this elegant aircraft.

FE.2B LATE

'Jess', G&J Weir built, 100 Sqn and USAS, mid-late 1918

Jeroen Veen

I HAVE TO ADMIT THAT THE WINGNUT WINGS FE.2B ALWAYS LOOKED A BIT DAUNTING ON ME AND SINCE I DIDN'T HAVE MUCH EXPERIENCE WITH WW1 PLANES IT WAS DEFINATELY NOT BE THE FIRST KIT FROM THIS ERA TO TACKLE.

That didn't have anything to do with the quality of the kit. It is well known how good the WnW kits are. It was just that the incredible amount of rigging seemed to great a challenge to tackle. But after the Gotha, Fokker and Hisso I felt comfortable enough and this book seemed the perfect opportunity to give this kit a go.

The FE.2b arrived at the front in late 1915. It was a push engine machine, designed that way for a wide and unhindered field of fire. It was powered by a 120hp Austro-Daimler engine which was built by Beardmore, and it carried a crew of two. It definately wasn't the most beautiful plane of its time and it was relatively big, but it proved to be very effective. It was used for escort, reconnaissance, training and bombing duties. It was that last role that attracted me to this kit, and especially the fact that I could build 'Jess' which was painted all black but faded to a gray, which made painting this kit all the more interesting.

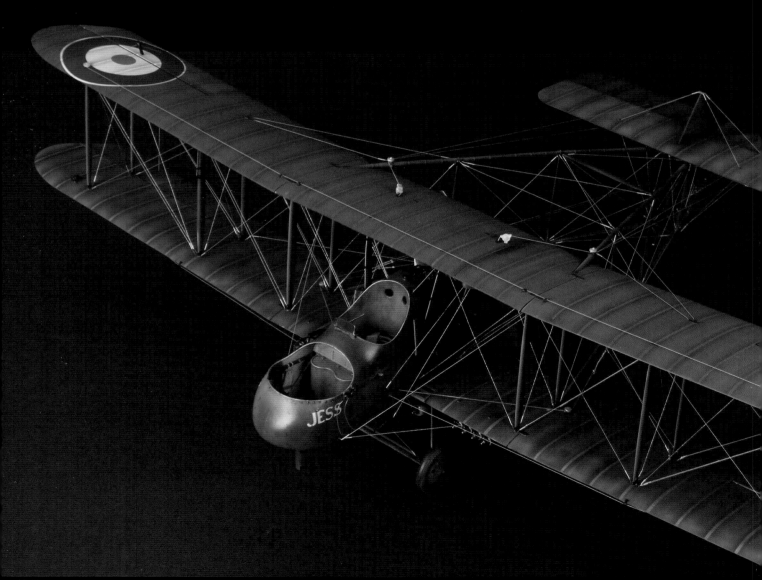

The Wingnuts Kit

The kit holds 11 plastic sprues, a photo etch frame, 3 sheets for the decals and an instruction booklet. If you are familiar with the WnW kits you know how good and well detailed they are and how much better they have become with their latest releases. This kit ranks as one of the best to me personally, with excellent fit and beautiful detail. There are some slight variations between the different schemes as well as some very nice options you can choose from. There are subtle differences in the cockpit layout, armament, engine, wingstruts, fuel tanks and propellor. Then there are various MG's and bombs of all sorts, and you get to decide if you want to install a camera in the nose section or not.

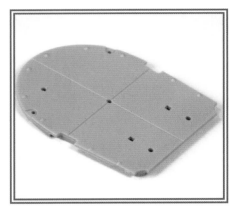

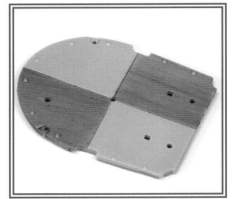

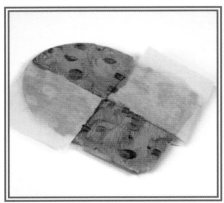

Beginning with the cockpit assembly, the floor panel of the cockpit seems a good place to show you how I paint woordgrain. The whole proces starts with a basecoat of Tamiya Tan. A sandcolor would work very good as well. The entire panel is airbrushed in this color and sealed with a coat of Semi Gloss Varnish. This is left to harden out completely. I think that one of the secrets of painting convincing wood patterns is to

treat each panel seperately. Two of the panels are masked. The panels then receive a coat of Raw Umber and Burnt Sienna oil paints. This is dabbed on liberally in a random fashion. I then take an old wide dry brush and start pulling it through the oil paint. Clean the brush regularly on a piece of paper and don't moisten it with thinner. By repeating the process the grain pattern will slowly

but surely appear.
After the painted parts are dry another coat of Semi Gloss Varnish is applied. After this is dry the panels that are painted now are masked and the whole process is repeated on the unpainted panels. By varying the direction of the woodgrain you can emphasize the different structures and panels.

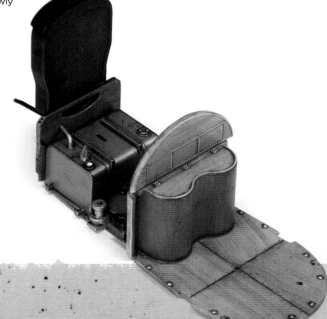

The floorpanel is almost done. After the Semi Gloss Varnish is dried out there's only one thing left to do: application of washes, just as you would do on your usual paintwork. In this case I only added a thin wash to emphasize the panellines. The whole proces takes some time, but is easy to do and leaves you with a convincing result.

THE COCKPIT AND INTERIOR

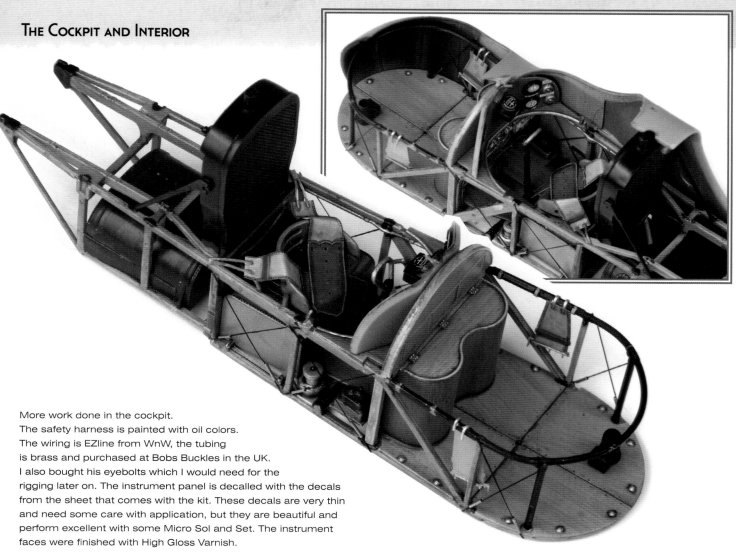

More work done in the cockpit.
The safety harness is painted with oil colors.
The wiring is EZline from WnW, the tubing
is brass and purchased at Bobs Buckles in the UK.
I also bought his eyebolts which I would need for the
rigging later on. The instrument panel is decalled with the decals
from the sheet that comes with the kit. These decals are very thin
and need some care with application, but they are beautiful and
perform excellent with some Micro Sol and Set. The instrument
faces were finished with High Gloss Varnish.

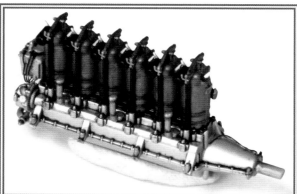

THE BEARDMORE ENGINE

The parts WnW offers are superbly detailed and the moulds
are as clean as they come. The engine is very exposed in
the fuselage and clearly visible. That is why I added some
etchings from the HGW-set that is specifically designed for
this kit.

The painting of the engine required copper and brass
colours, most of it is applied by airbrush but the smaller
details are brush painted of course. Tamiya Transparent
Yellow is used to create some colour differences between

the copper and brass. The details received a wash with diluted Tamiya Smoke, which gives a nice subtle depth around the details. Everything was sealed for protection with Tamiya Gloss Varnish.

I added some grime and oil stains from AK Interactive . These are fine products, but you could achieve a similar affect with oil paints. After all was painted the engine was sealed with Tamiya Semi Gloss Varnish.

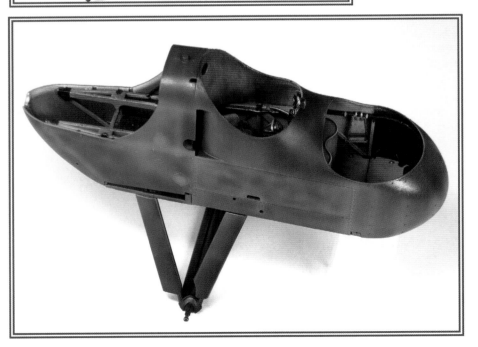

Night Colours

Early on I decided I wanted to do the nightbomber version of the FE.2b. The kit offers two options, one of which being Jess. Jess carried a faded black paintscheme, so I started of with airbrushing the fuselage entirely with Tamiya Rubber Black. After the Black had dried I took a gloss Dark Gray, thinned it down considerably and started building up color with an airbrush. I really like working with highly diluted paints. Not only do they spray well but they give you great control over color density. I gradually built up the colors untill it looked something like this.

The first step in the weathering proces: breaking the color. I did this by adding small dots of oil paint randomly over the fuselage. Colors chosen are white, grey, ochre and some brown. These were left to settle for 15 minutes. After that, with a wide soft brush moistened with thinner I started to fade the dots into a striping effect. The effect looks rather stark here but will become less strong during the the weathering that is to follow. You can also see that I try to differentiate between materials by using different varnishes. Most of the fuselage was done with Tamiya Semi Gloss Varnish, but the canvas sides were done with Tamiya Matt Varnish.

A light wash of diluted Raw Umber oil paint was applied around the details. The wheels were lightly drybrushed after they were painted and a wash was added. The mud splashes were done with a piece of sponge and some Humbrol Matt 29 Dark Earth. This is lightly dabbed on the tyres and hub. I was really pleased with the effects achieved. The curved part behind the pilot seat caused me all sorts of problems. This is not a seperate panel and needs to be completely blended in with the sidepanels.

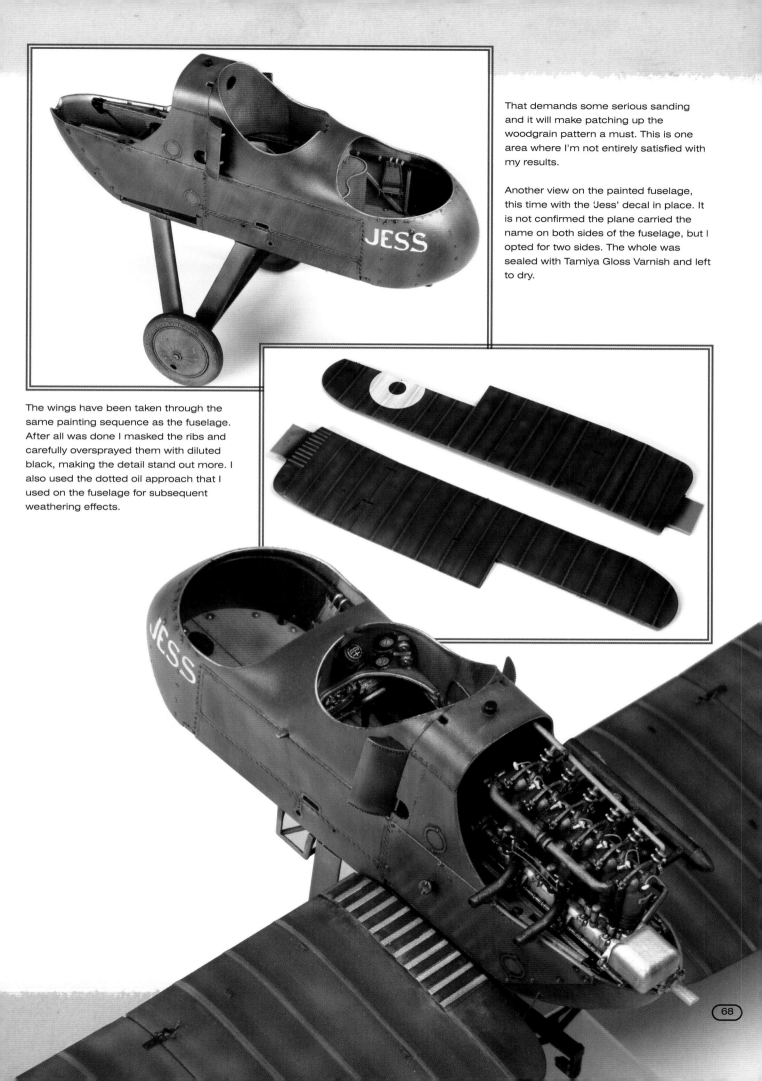

That demands some serious sanding and it will make patching up the woodgrain pattern a must. This is one area where I'm not entirely satisfied with my results.

Another view on the painted fuselage, this time with the 'Jess' decal in place. It is not confirmed the plane carried the name on both sides of the fuselage, but I opted for two sides. The whole was sealed with Tamiya Gloss Varnish and left to dry.

The wings have been taken through the same painting sequence as the fuselage. After all was done I masked the ribs and carefully oversprayed them with diluted black, making the detail stand out more. I also used the dotted oil approach that I used on the fuselage for subsequent weathering effects.

The carrier for the 112lb bomb was painted and installed in place. I drilled out the tiny holes so I could attach the cables that are done with fishing wire. Again, brass tubing from Bobs Buckles was used for the job. This is a somewhat complex step in the building process because the instructions do not show very clearly where everything should go. A quick google search on the internet solved all the problems quickly though.

The eyelets from Bobs Buckles. I carefully drilled out the holes in the wings and then dipped the eyelet in some cyano. It is then fixed in place. Beware! Make sure the tiny loop isn't clogged with glue because you will not be able to attach the wires. Check this during this phase because you will have problems if you need to replace the eyelet later on! When you spoil glue on the paintwork of the wing some Matt Varnish will solve the problem. Perferably make this correction after the wires are installed.

The dotted oil technique briefly explained. On the wing on top of this photo you see the random application of oil dots. I pick the colors by trying to picture the end result. Lighter colors for a bleached effect, darker colors for some more depth in the paintwork, or a balance between the two. The middle part shows the start of the blending process. With a moist (not wet) wide soft brush I start making stripes in the direction of the airflow. Make sure you create stripes, don't blend all the colors together.

The last part shows how the effect should look when you're done. After this has dried seal it with a Varnish of your choice to protect the work done so far.

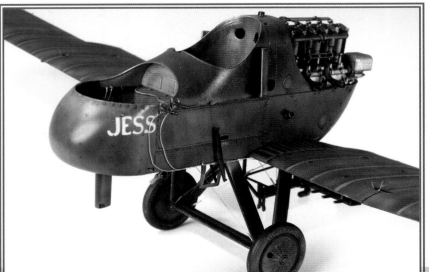

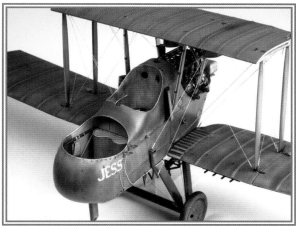

I deviated a little from the instructions. WnW tells you to install the three part top wing as a whole, but I didn't want to align all the struts in one go, fearing that I might leave a mess doing so. I therefor started with installing the centre top wing. This also made it easier to start the rigging process because everything can be reached so much better. The two outer parts of the wing are installed and rigged. I treated this whole structure as a model in itself. It was completely finished, painted and rigged before I started on the tailsection. She's definately starting to look like an FE.2b now, and for the first time you get some feeling for the sheer size of the plane. It is big!

The bombs are attached to their racks. I painted these Tamiya Yellow Green. The green and red bands are decals from the sheet. Everything was sealed with a coat of gloss varnish. Light washes of brown oil paints and some light dabbing of Humbrol Matt 29 Dark Earth with a sponge are good for the weathering. I think the bombs give a nice dash of color to the otherwise dark grey and green plane.

The tailsection also was treated like a model in itself. It was painted with the techniques described earlier and completely rigged separately. It can then be attached to the front section of the plane so avoiding having to handle the entire aircraft. Once in place any final connecting wires were attached. I made sure to scrape away the paint on the mating surfaces where the booms are connected to the wings, otherwise they won't fit. After rigging a total of some 250 wires I was extremely happy to see her finally complete!

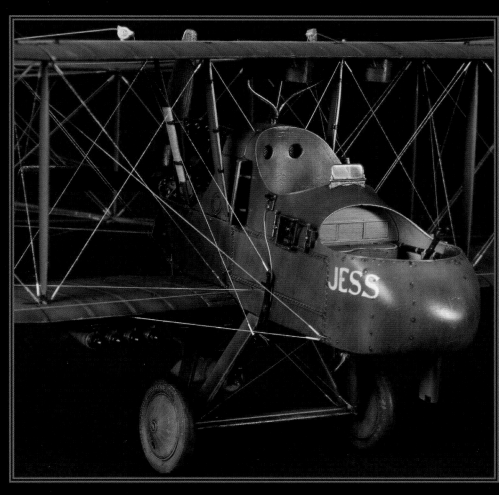

This kit really is a boy's dream but it takes a modeller with some skill to actually build it. If you have some experience with rigging and building kits this size I would definately recommend this one to you. With some patience you will have a beautiful addition to your model collection!

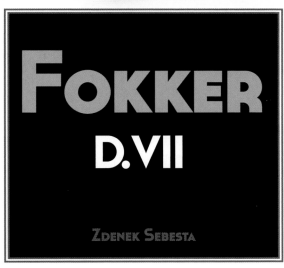

FOKKER
D.VII

ZDENEK SEBESTA

WINGNUT WINGS OFFERS THIS FAMOUS GERMAN WWI FIGHTER IN THREE DIFFERENT VERSIONS, CORRESPONDING TO THE ACTUAL AIRCRAFT MANUFACTURERS: FOKKER, ALBATROS AND OAW.

From all the possible colour schemes available I settled on building an OAW-manufactured example because I wanted to build the aircraft known as "Die Sieben Schwaben" (The Seven Swabians), based on a story from Grimm's Fairy Tales. This particular aircraft flew with Jasta 65 in 1918 and was piloted by Wilhelm Scheutzel. Though not a long or notable fighting career, with both sides of the fuselage dominated by large, colourful, characters taken from the Fairy Tale, I found this most appealing. The scheme decals are from a Wingnut Wings decal set sold separately.

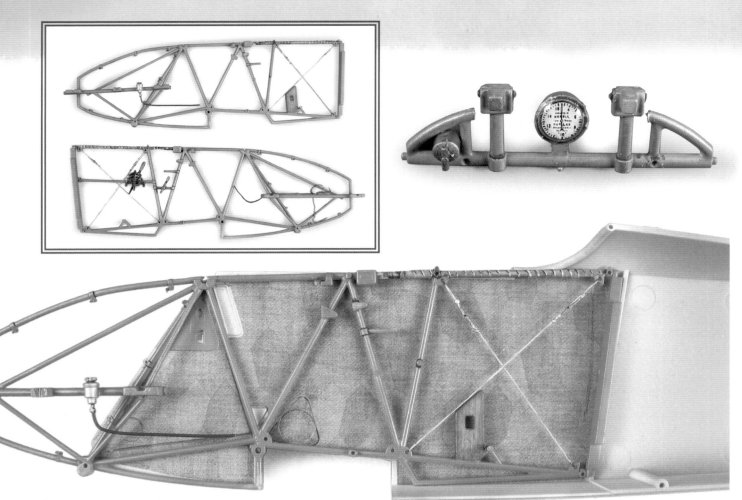

The Cockpit and Interior

The cockpit supplied with this Wingnut Wings kit is very well detailed. I did however add a few additional parts from the HGW sets; instrument frames and the fabric seatbelts which significantly improved the overall look. The cross bracing of the internal fuselage structure is also offered as part of the HGW photo-etched interior detailing set but I preferred to use the elastic 'EZ line' instead. On the original aircraft, the cockpit floor and instrument panel were made from varnished wood. These are easily replicated thanks to the wood-finish decals that are also available from HGW.

I glued on the dashboard, the instrument frames and the switches in their respective positions. The instrument dials are part of the decal.

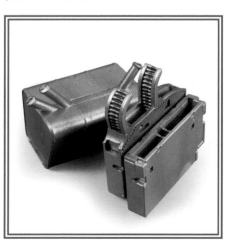

I always like to enhance my models by either modifying or opening up access panels, rather than just building them out-of-the-box. The Wingnut Wings kits are limited in this area, however the level of detail and overall quality still make them the best on the market. One area that can be exposed is the engine. The Mercedes D.III engine that comes with the kit is well finished but I still decided to improve this with the replacement of some of the engine body screws using resin ones available from a 'Calibre 35' set.

Other accessories came from the Polish company 'Taurus' and greatly enhance the overall appearance of the engine; the lifters with covers and springs. These items may be small but the surface detail is to a very high level. Taurus even offer drain valves for each cylinder, however I chose to use the resin drain valves from the British company Aviattic at the time I was building my model. Apart from the addition of a few leads and cables from copper wire, the finished engine was then ready for painting. The instructions supplied thoroughly cover the respective colours of the various parts and even include a number of detailed photographs of the actual aircraft.
Due to the fact that the model can be built to represent

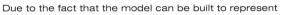

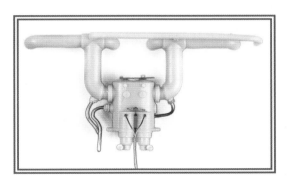

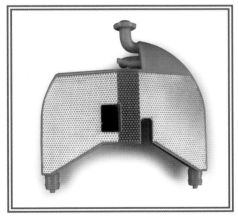

aircraft manufactured by the various companies, there are several variations of radiator and engine cowlings as well as decals available. For this reason it is vitally important that the modeller chooses their version prior to commencing the build and sticks strictly to the instructions to avoid any mistakes. Another supplementary part available from the company RB Productions is an etched radiator grill that has the correct profile. This was found to be a perfect fit to the kit parts and I installed it using the extra thin Alteco superglue.

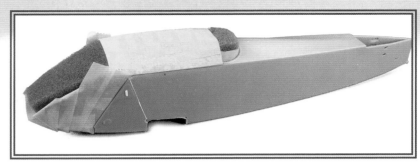

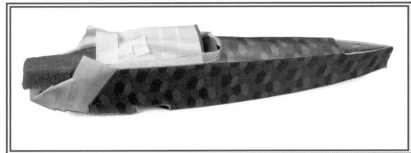

Surface finishes

Wood and canvas formed the majority of WWI airframe construction. When manufactured, the Fokker D.VIIs were almost entirely covered in lozenge-printed canvas apart from the engine cowlings, undercarriage and vertical tail surfaces. Like many aircraft serving in the Jastas, my chosen aircraft "The Seven Swabians" was personalised with the fuselage fabric being re-painted in a medium grey, and both the engine covers and horizontal tail surfaces receiving a reddish-brown finish. Once the basic model was completed, I sprayed the entire aircraft with a coat of MR. Paint white primer. To enhance the areas around the rib tapes, I applied a highly diluted coat of black to provide some basic shading, followed by a thin coat of varnish, before I applied the lozenge fabric decals.

These aircraft were manufactured with either four-colour or five colour lozenge-patterned fabric, with a lighter coloured cloth applied to the undersurfaces. There are various model companies offering these fabric prints as decals, however I chose to use those available from the British company Aviattic. This company not only offer pre-shaped lozenge-patterned decals specifically for the Wingnut Wings Fokker D.VII, which can be directly applied to the individual surfaces (e.g. wings, ailerons, etc.), but offer a choice of factory finish,

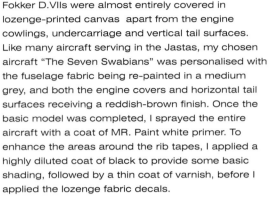

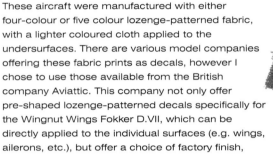

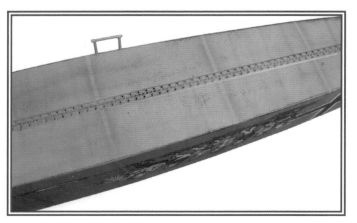

faded or brown varnished. On top of this, the modeller can even choose what colour ribbing tapes from pale blue, pink or lozenge-patterned fabric, thereby giving a wide choice on how the finished model might look. I chose to use the Aviattic four-colour lozenge with the pale blue ribbing tapes for my model. Even though the ribbing tapes are printed integral with the main fabric decals, they lined up perfectly with the surface detail on the wings. Additionally, the transparent carrier film used on these decals was very flexible and strong enough to stretch as much as a millimetre or so to ensure accurate positioning without damage.

For the fuselage and tail, I proceeded as per the basic model instructions – only the vertical tail surfaces were left uncovered in the MR. Paint white primer. With the exception of the engine covers, I applied the supplied lozenge decals to the entire fuselage assembly. Obviously there was a variation in colour between the Aviattic decals I applied to the wings and those of the model that I

applied to the fuselage. In my case this didn't matter as on the second day after a thorough drying, I sprayed thin layers of MR. Paint blue-grey (MRP 038) to the fuselage and a reddish-brown (80% MRP 029 + 20% MRP 052) to the horizontal tail surfaces. It is very important to spray each thin layer under constant control so as not to completely obliterate the underneath lozenge pattern – far more interesting than just covering these surfaces with a sprayed solid colour. Likewise to replicate wear-and-tear in service, I scraped away some areas of the paint to expose the lozenge fabric underneath.

The wings and tail surfaces are nicely detailed with rib tape and stitching detail, replicating that of the original aircraft. All moveable control surfaces are supplied as separate items, enabling the modeller to deflect these from the neutral position on their finished model. The leather bushings for the control surface push rods, along with the stitching applied to the underside of the fuselage came from the HGW supplementary set. The bushings were painted with a leather colour and individually applied after the model had been painted.

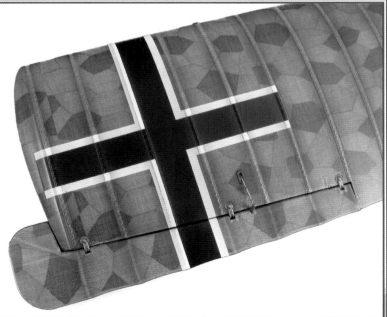

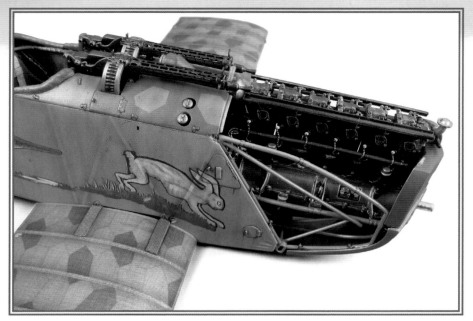

Next the engine covers were painted in the reddish-brown colour I had pre-mixed, then the undercarriage and the sheet metal panelling of the forward fuselage were painted with a colour combination of green (GSI C 302) and purple (GSI H 39). At this point the model was given an overall finish of MR. Paint gloss varnish (MRP 048) prior to the application of the main scheme decals. The decals supplied with the kit, as well as the "Die Sieben Schwaben" scheme markings, which came from the separate Wingnut Wings decal set 'Fighting Fokkers– part 4/cat. No.30009' are of excellent quality and printed, as usual, by Cartograf. To achieve a perfect registry of the decals to the fine surface detail of the model, I used the GSI solutions Mr. Mark Setter and Softener. Decals now in place and thoroughly dried, I repainted the whole aircraft with a coat of semi-matt varnish, followed by a wash to highlight some surface detail using MIG Production Dark and Neutral Wash solutions.

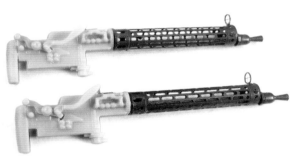

The Fokker D.VII aircraft were armed with two Spandau machine guns synchronised to fire through the propeller arc. The basic kit offers two versions; one all plastic, the other with a photo-etched perforated jacket. However the best overall option is a set of turned brass barrels available from the Polish manufacturer Master, which is the option I went for. The aftermarket manufacturing company Uschi van Der Rosten offers a chemical treatment solution that enables the brass parts to be given a durable black gunmetal-type finish.

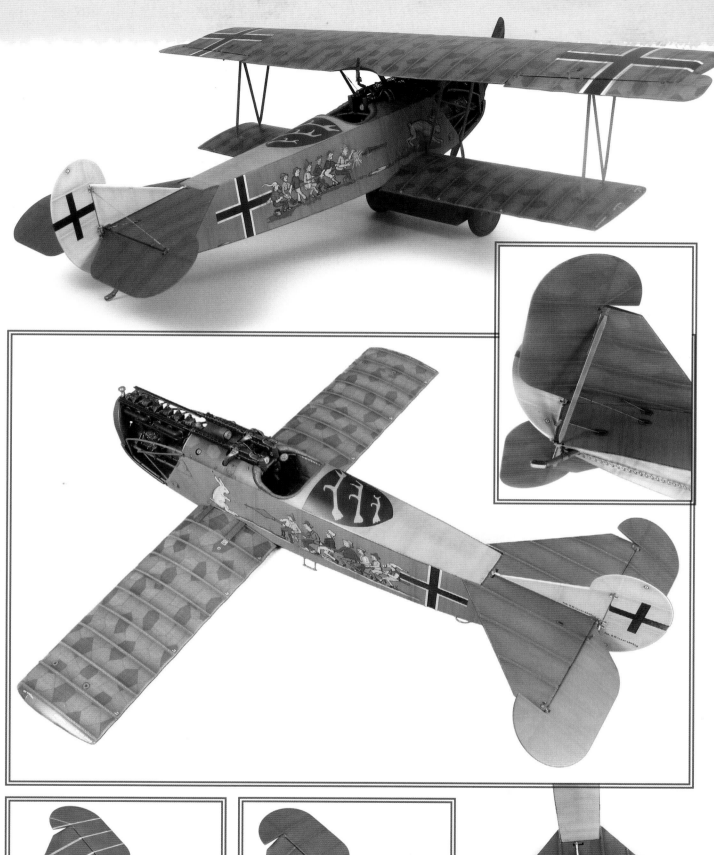

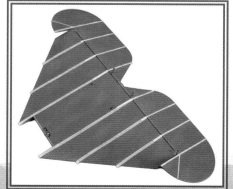

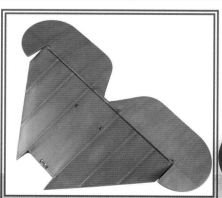

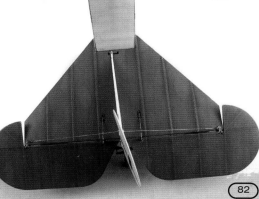

THE PROPELLER

Models in this scale will always benefit from a scale wooden propeller. Several propeller types were fitted to Fokker D.VII; in the case of my chosen aircraft, a Niendorf was fitted. The Czech manufacturer PEJE-Models reproduces scale laminated wooden propellers for virtually all the Wingnut Wings kit range. I carefully cut off the propeller boss from the plastic propeller supplied with the kit, sprayed with metallic paint and glued it onto the wooden PEJE-Models propeller. Finally I airbrushed the complete assembly with semi-gloss varnish – the original gloss finish looked too new. The Niendorf propellers only carried simple black information lettering and small company logos on the front of each blade.

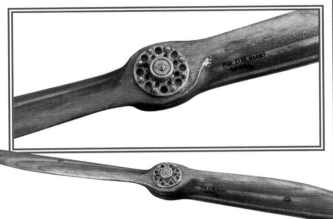

THE FINAL CONSTRUCTION

The final construction necessary to complete the model was to attach the upper wing and undercarriage assemblies using the well-fitting struts and braces. The rigid design of the Fokker D.VII meant that the airframe required very few external cross-bracing wires, except for those attached to the main undercarriage and the vertical tail surfaces. The only other visible cables are those used to operate the various control surfaces.

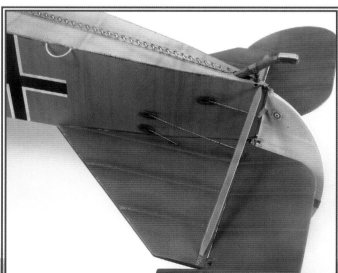

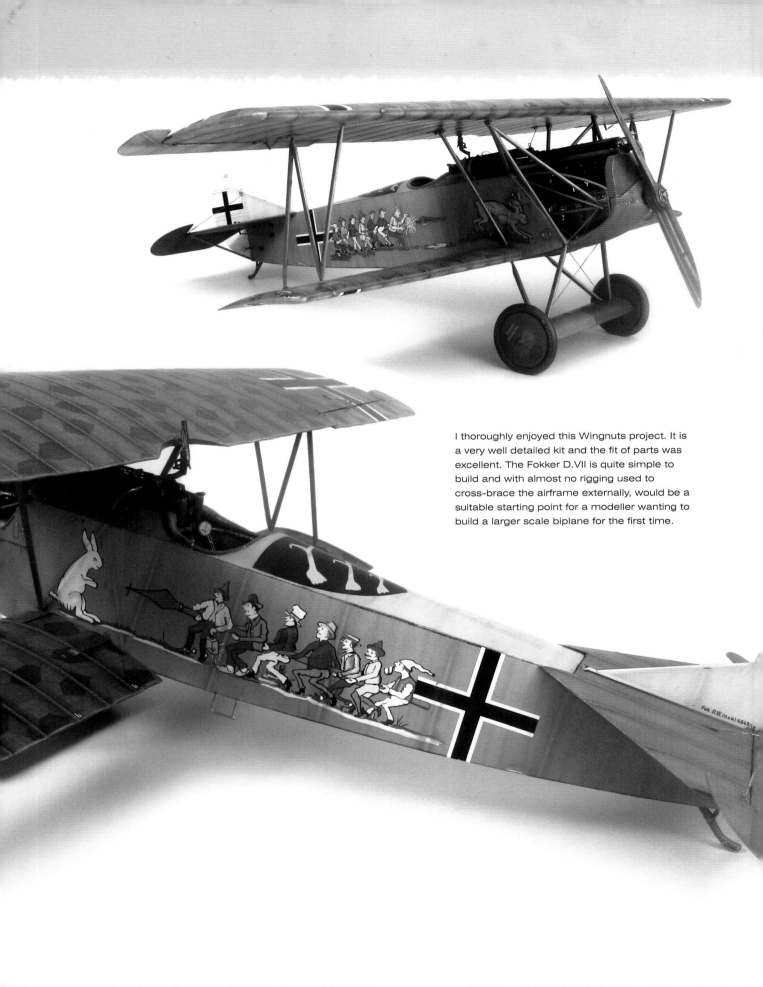

I thoroughly enjoyed this Wingnuts project. It is a very well detailed kit and the fit of parts was excellent. The Fokker D.VII is quite simple to build and with almost no rigging used to cross-brace the airframe externally, would be a suitable starting point for a modeller wanting to build a larger scale biplane for the first time.

Sopwith TRIPLANE

MICHAEL GRUSON

The Sopwth Triplane, developed from the Sopwith Pup, with the addition of a third wing giving it peerless handling. A total of 150 Triplanes were built. It quickly caused a sensation, with German pilots preferring not to commit to combat at the mere sight of this very agile hunter. For several reasons, its frontline service career was quite short before its place was taken by the famous Sopwith Camel. A few examples, a total of 16, were used by the Centre D'Aviation Maritime headquarted in Saint-Pol-Sur-Mer before it was replaced with the Spad VII.

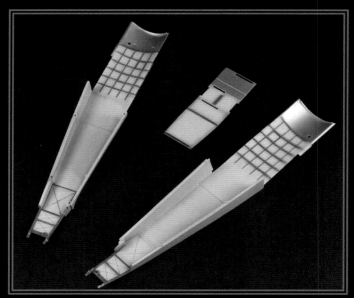

COCKPIT AND ENGINE

The inside of the fuselage is stunning : the engine, the fuel tank, radiators pipes are all depicted, nothing is missing! You can almost make a stand alone model of the interior parts. Once the elements have been pre-painted, the assembly is easy provided you make sure that each part takes its exct place. The complxity of the subject means that the tollerances are always exact and any error will effect the fit inside the fuselage. I used oil paint applied over an acrylic base coat to create the woodgrain finish of the cockpit parts. Dragging the wet oil colour with a brush creates a pleasing grained effect, especially visible on the large main struts on each side of the cockpit. I also added the cockpit rigging wires using elastic line and I used the kit seat belts which I bent to a natural-looking draped position over the seat.

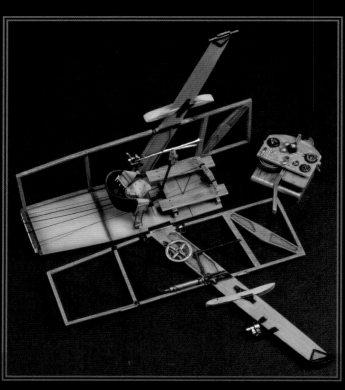

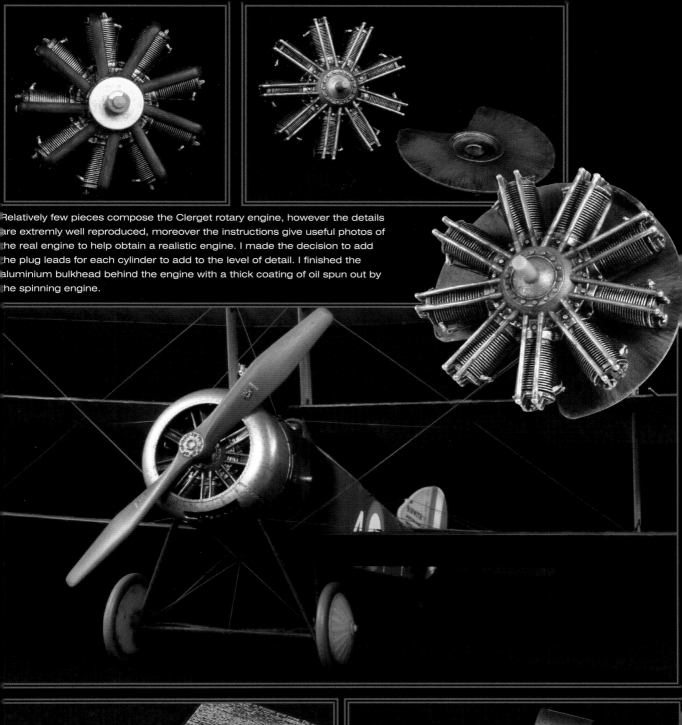

Relatively few pieces compose the Clerget rotary engine, however the details are extremely well reproduced, moreover the instructions give useful photos of the real engine to help obtain a realistic engine. I made the decision to add the plug leads for each cylinder to add to the level of detail. I finished the aluminium bulkhead behind the engine with a thick coating of oil spun out by the spinning engine.

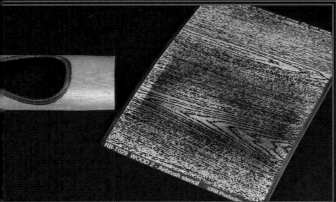

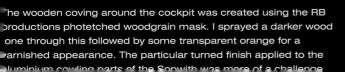

The wooden coving around the cockpit was created using the RB productions photetched woodgrain mask. I sprayed a darker wood one through this followed by some transparent orange for a varnished appearance. The particular turned finish applied to the aluminium cowling parts of the Sopwith was more of a challenge to replicate. I used Rub 'n buff aluminium to create the base aluminium finish and then I applied the circular marks over this using a wooden cocktail stick with a flattened tip to apply the aluminium paint. I rotated the stick on the panels to give a turned effect to each mark.

PAINTING AND WEATHERING

The instructions gives us a choice between two colorus: the greenish PC10 or the brownish PC12... I decided in favor of the PC10. To reproduce this I decided to use Gunze H 303 as a base to which I added a touch of brown. This mixture was sprayed over the the upper surfaces of the kit. The colour was then worked over to give more realism by emphasizing the structural elements under the fabric. This work will be localised using targeted sprays of highlighting tones along the masking tape strips carefully applied over the raised details. I started with Gunze H 79 Sandy Yellow sprayed on the upper parts, which are the most exposed to the light. Conversely, all the lower parts are darkened thanks to very light sprays along the masking tape now hiding the previous clear

PATINA

spraying.
I chose to add some more weathering effects mainly using oil paints. Four colours were used: White, Naples Yellow, Burnt Umber and Black. Their application was done with a brush without any thinning and then blending them. They are ideal because they can be worked without a hurry, mixed and blended and the degree of opacity can be controlled using a cotton bud to lift off paint or clean it away completely. The process is quite long but it brings more character to the model.

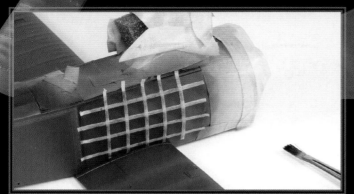

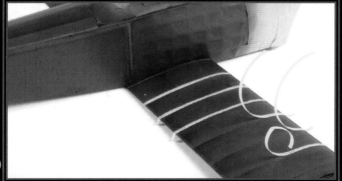

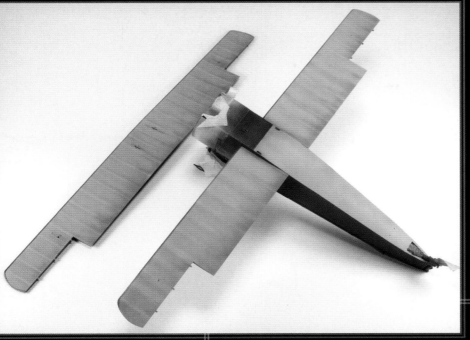

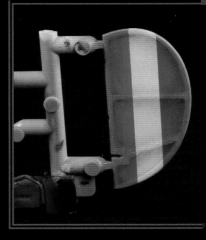

The same weathing process was also used to finish the linen undersides.

The stages of the oil colour weathering can clearly be seen in this image of some of the wings during the process.

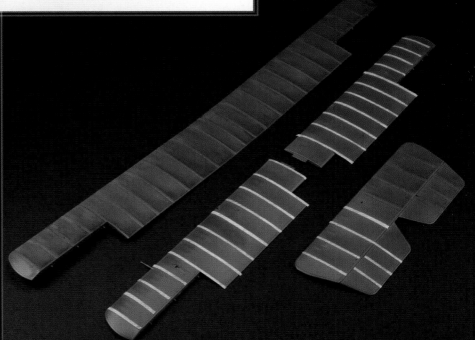

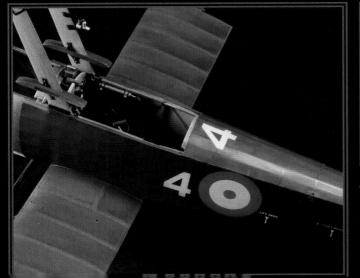

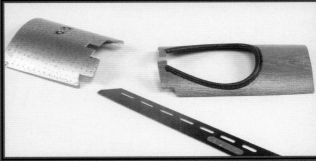

To ease the fitting of the cockpit surrounds I cut the front cowling section from the wooden part, something that is required in any case if using the twin Vickers MG installation.

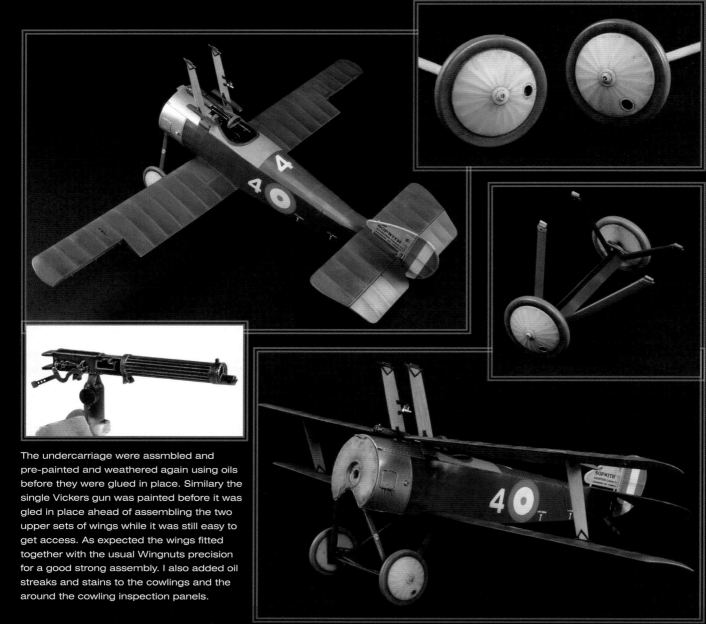

The undercarriage were assmbled and pre-painted and weathered again using oils before they were glued in place. Similary the single Vickers gun was painted before it was gled in place ahead of assembling the two upper sets of wings while it was still easy to get access. As expected the wings fitted together with the usual Wingnuts precision for a good strong assembly. I also added oil streaks and stains to the cowlings and the around the cowling inspection panels.

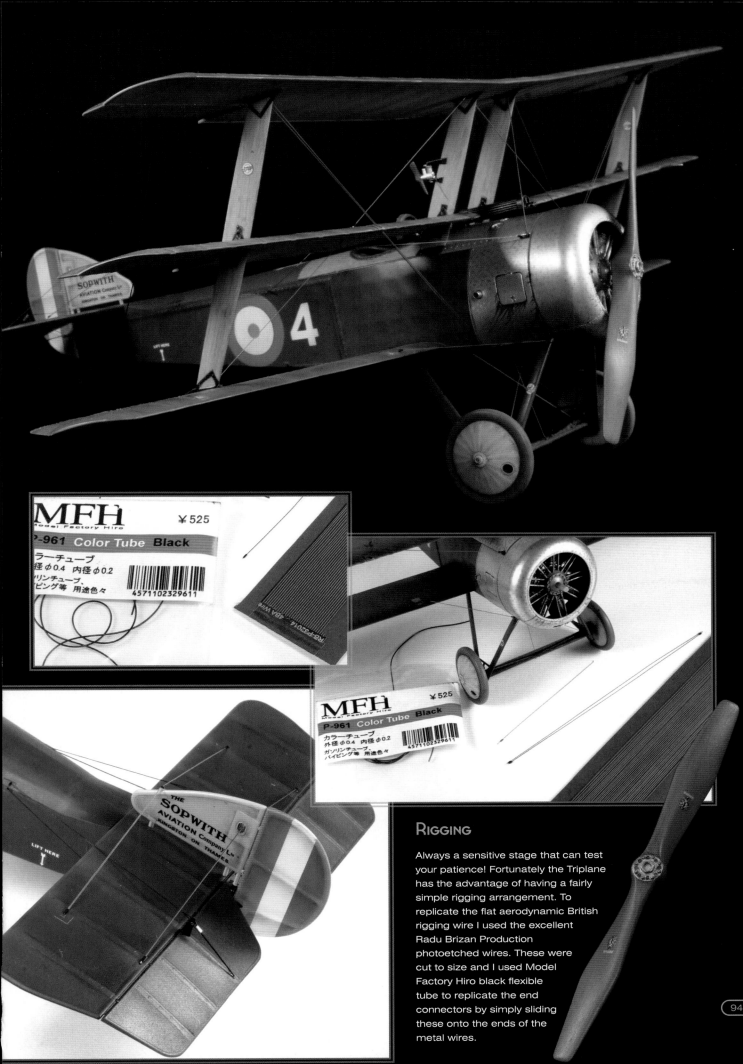

MFH Model Factory Hiro ¥525
P-961 Color Tube Black
カラーチューブ
外径 φ0.4 内径 φ0.2
ガソリンチューブ、
パイピング等 用途色々
4571102329611

MFH Model Factory Hiro ¥525
P-961 Color Tube Black
カラーチューブ
外径 φ0.4 内径 φ0.2
ガソリンチューブ、
パイピング等 用途色々
4571102329611

RIGGING

Always a sensitive stage that can test your patience! Fortunately the Triplane has the advantage of having a fairly simple rigging arrangement. To replicate the flat aerodynamic British rigging wire I used the excellent Radu Brizan Production photoetched wires. These were cut to size and I used Model Factory Hiro black flexible tube to replicate the end connectors by simply sliding these onto the ends of the metal wires.

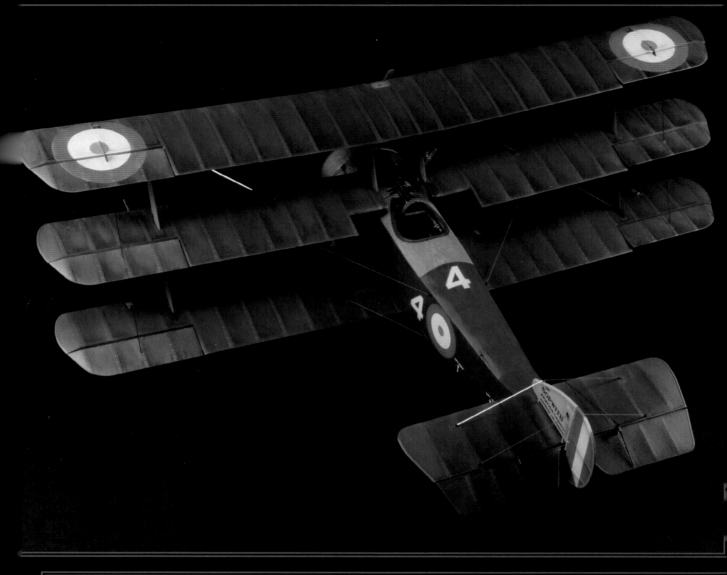

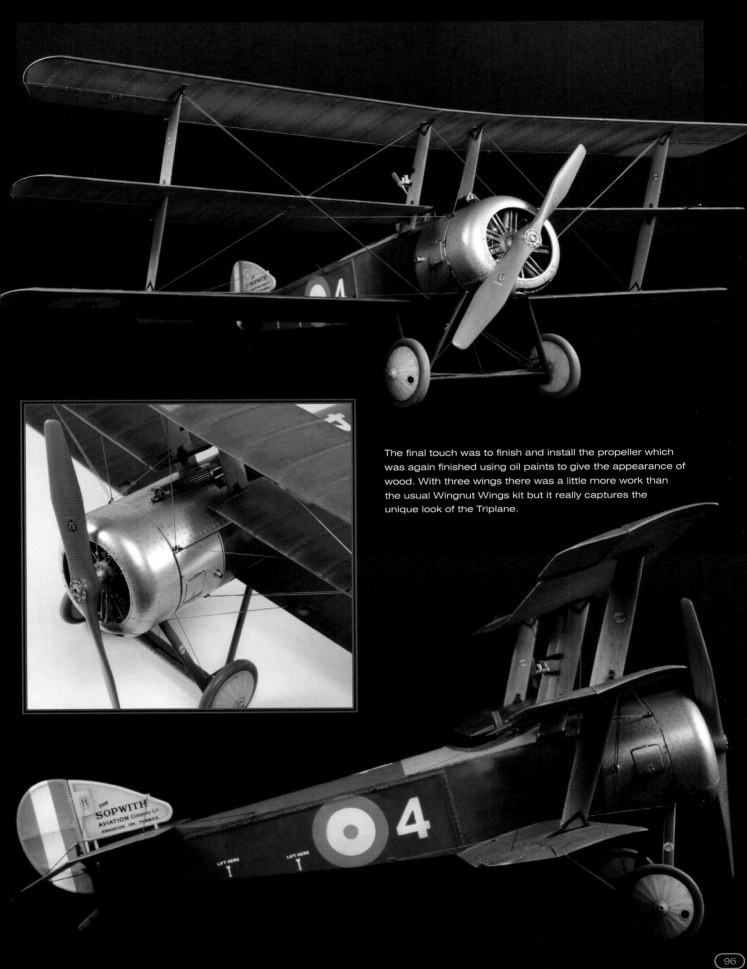

The final touch was to finish and install the propeller which was again finished using oil paints to give the appearance of wood. With three wings there was a little more work than the usual Wingnut Wings kit but it really captures the unique look of the Triplane.

PFALZ D.IIIA

DAVID PARKER

SURELY ONE OF THE SLEEKEST AND MOST ELEGANT DESIGNS OF ALL THE FIGHTERS OF THE ERA, THE PFALZ D.IIIA ALSO OFFERS A WIDE CHOICE OF COLOUR SCHEMES.

For me the stunning Jasta 30 aircraft with their variations around the big orange diamond Staffel markings were immediately appealing. In particular the aircraft flown by Ltn. Hans-Georg von der Marwitz which carried only the diamond markings on the factory sliver grey, a scheme which complimented the sleek lines of the aircraft, giving it a very modern look.

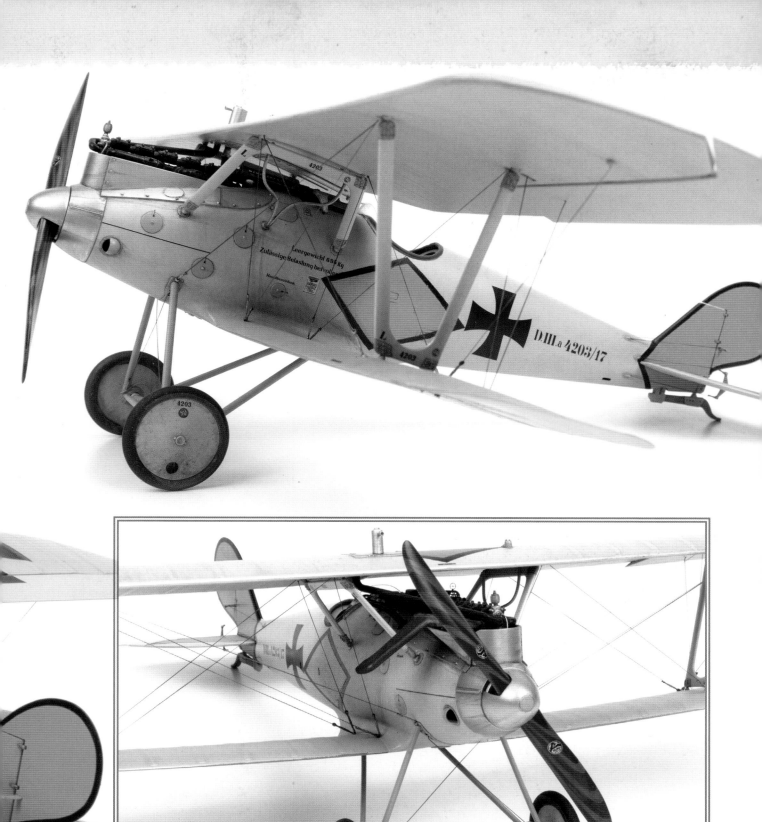

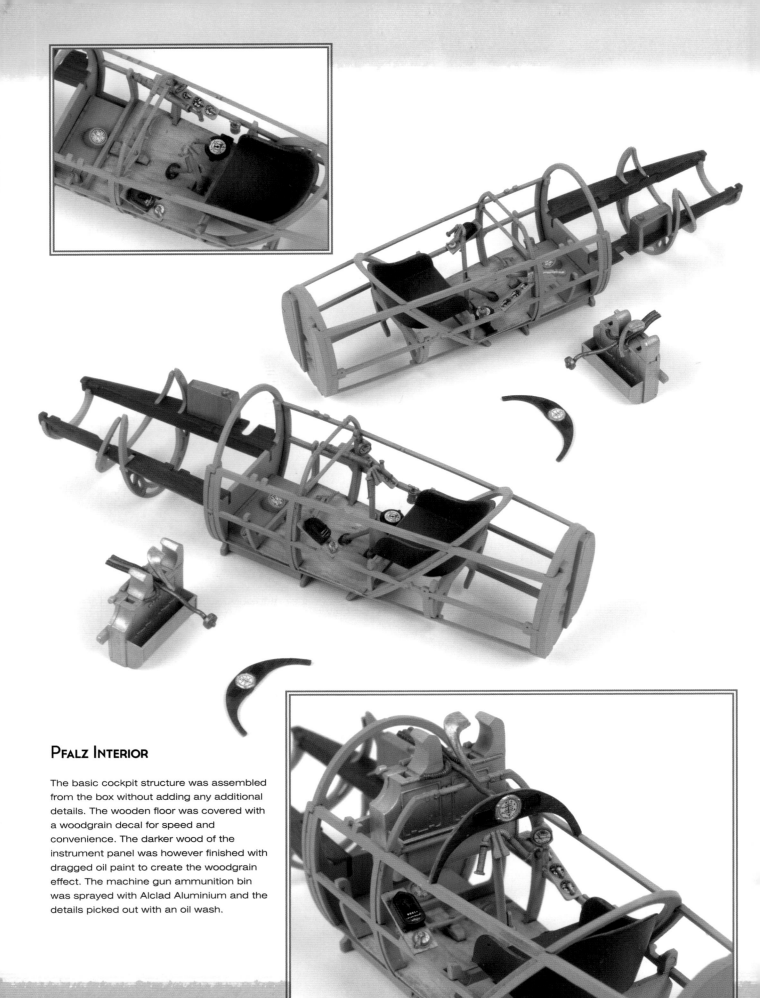

PFALZ INTERIOR

The basic cockpit structure was assembled
from the box without adding any additional
details. The wooden floor was covered with
a woodgrain decal for speed and
convenience. The darker wood of the
instrument panel was however finished with
dragged oil paint to create the woodgrain
effect. The machine gun ammunition bin
was sprayed with Alclad Aluminium and the
details picked out with an oil wash.

The basis of the engine is assembled and painted with a pale grey wash over the aluminium engine block to give a tarnished appearance. Plastic rod spark plugs are added along with lead wire spark plug leads.

The spark plug leads are connected to the pipe work running across the cylinders and this is repeated on both sides.

The bundle of electrical cables from the distributor cap is also added using lead wire because it is so easy to manipluate.

The opposite side of the engine note that all the bolt heads on the crank case have been picked out in steel.

The final stage is weather the engine using grey/brown washes over the black areas and applying layers of oil staining to the lower parts. Given how little of the engine is visible with the cowlings in place the detail and finishing here is more than adequate.

The completed engine is mounted in place on the rest of the internal structure before the last internal details are completed and the fuselage closed.

Making the most of the kit seatbelts. There are aftermarket seatbelts available but the photoetched kit parts can work just as well with some careful paintwork. I began by carefully shaping the belts to conform to the seat, trying to achieve a natural drooped position. The belts were sprayed with a pale linen colour. shading was

applied around the buckles and clasps and lines of stitching were painted with a fine brush. The buckles and clasps were painted with interior grey/green and a thin oil wash was used to define these and to add shadows to the belts. The finished belts were then fitted into the cockpit.

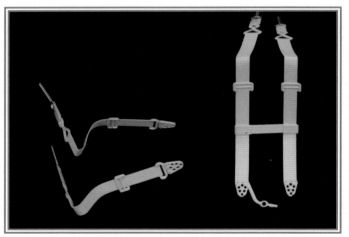

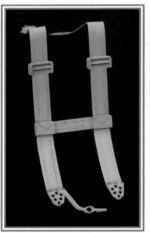

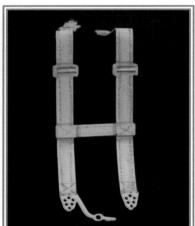

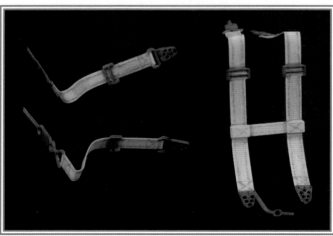

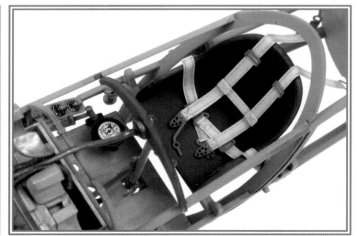

The twin Spandau guns use the kit photoetched barrel sleeves and are finished using Mr Metal Color 'Dark Iron'. They are test fitted here but will be removed to avoid accidental damage when the fuselage is painted.

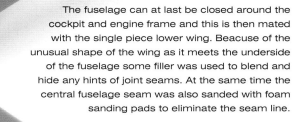

The fuselage can at last be closed around the cockpit and engine frame and this is then mated with the single piece lower wing. Beacuse of the unusual shape of the wing as it meets the underside of the fuselage some filler was used to blend and hide any hints of joint seams. At the same time the central fuselage seam was also sanded with foam sanding pads to eliminate the seam line.

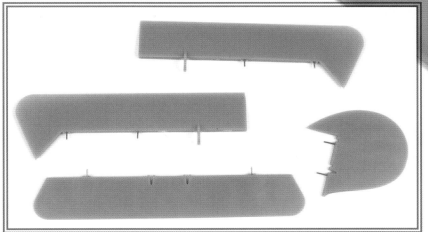

I took the time to drill and and add brass rod pins to all the control surfaces to strengthen the fixings which are otherwise quite fragile. Corresponding holes are then drilled in the fuselage and wings to accept the new pins.

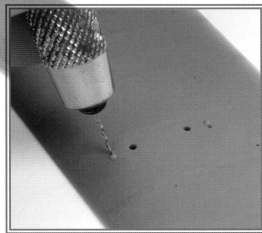

I also drilled all the location points for the rigging while they are still easily accessible.

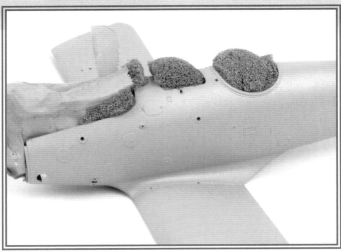

Pfalz Silver Grey

The interior parts were masked with tape and sponge to protect them during painting.

The unique factory-applied silver grey that the Pfalz was delivered in posed a particular challenge to paint. The period photos show this to have quite a pale tone with distinct reflective quality without being 'glittery' or liked a silver dope finish.

I began with a base coat of Misterkit GC17 'German Pfalz Silbergrau' acrylic paint. I then misted a thin coat of a pale aluminium over this to give the slight metallic sheen to the paint. There were a few repetitions using both colours to enhance or knock back the finish until I had a result that I thought was close to period photos.

The next stage was to start to distress the lovely paint finish I had just created by adding stains. Again the kit instructions provide excellent reference pictures that show the dirty fuselage around the engine and cockpit. I used thin acrylic washes applied using a sponge to impart an irregular discolouration.

I also used a brush to work over this in selected areas. The subtle shine of the original paint can still be seen beneath the dirty areas.

The finished effects recreating the assorted fluid spills and the effects of airflow and the angle of the fuselage on the ground.

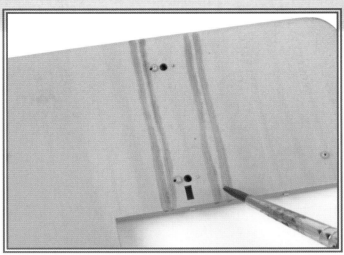

Moving to the wings I used an oil wash to dirty the surface by applying lines of wash each side of the rib tapes.

I used a flat brush with white spirit to drag and blend the lines working the the direction of airflow over the wing.

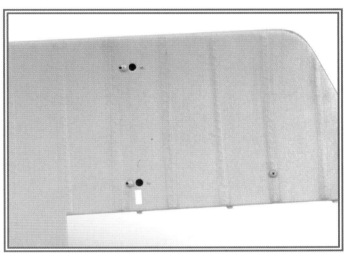

Repeatedly working over the area results in this very subtle finished effect.

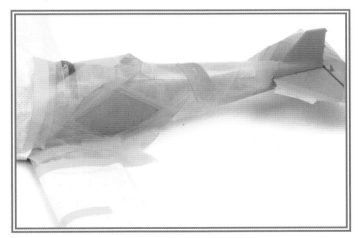

Jasta 30 Diamonds

At the time that the model was built there were no decals available for the dramatic Jasta 30 markings. The diamonds were masked out easily enough on the upper wing and tail but the curved fuselage sides were more problematic than I expected with some trial and error adjustments needed to get the shape correct. With everything masked I sprayed the glorious bright orange first. The centres of the diamonds were then masked and the black edges sprayed.

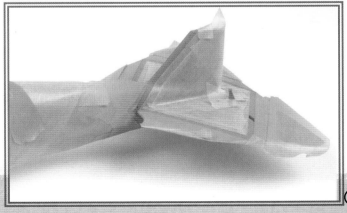

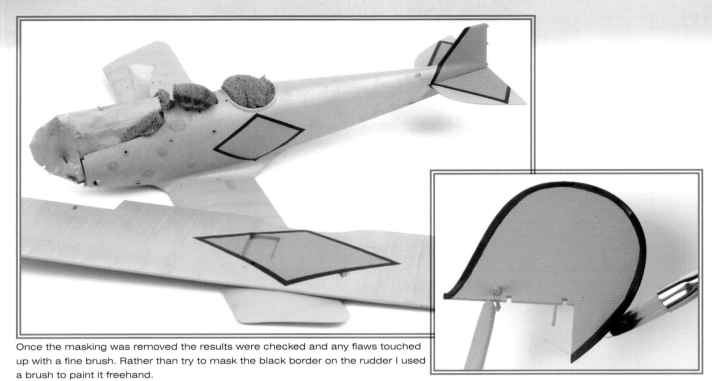

Once the masking was removed the results were checked and any flaws touched up with a fine brush. Rather than try to mask the black border on the rudder I used a brush to paint it freehand.

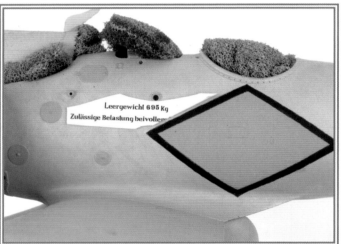

The factory applied weight designations on the fuselage have been overpainted by the unit markings so I trimmed the decals to fit against the diamond.

The other stencil decals were applied as well as the national markings. I had a problem with the aircraft registration number, and I adapted the kit decals along with some spare Pheon code numbers to create the correct number.

The masking was removed from the fuselage and a coat of satin varnish was applied. The cowling parts were fitted and these were initially painted using Alclad Aluminium but I then applied True Metal paste on top of the Alclad to enhance the bare metal finish.

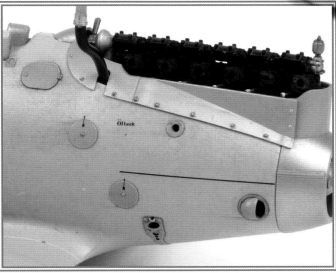

I used oil paint to apply streaking from the various inspection ports around the engine. This has the benefit of bieng easy to blend for a natural look. I also added oild stains to the engine cowlings using 502 Abteilung 'Engine Grease' oil colour.

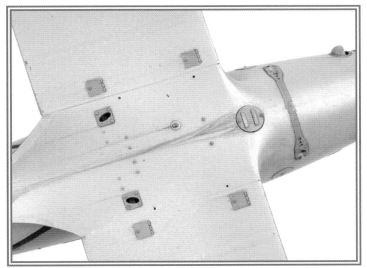

I applied oil stains to the underside of the fuselage from the drain point and inspection cover

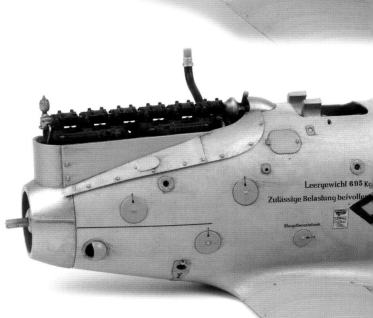

The progression of the staining on and around the nose can be seen in these pictures.

The Final Assembly Steps

The fuselage at this point is almost complete but it is important to finalise any details that will be hard or impossible to reach once the upper wing is fitted.
The twin Spandaus are therefore installed now using replacement turned brass barrel sleeves AM-32-023 from Master.

The guns were painted with Mr Metal Color 'Dark Iron' and mounted with their aluminium feed chutes.

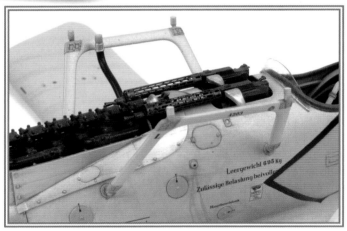

The central fuselage struts which have been pre-painted are then installed.

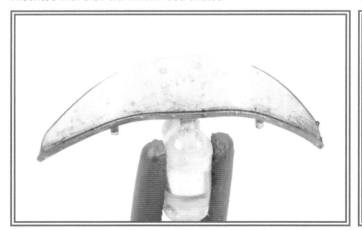

The windscreen is weathered with oil spatters from the engine and then fixed in position.

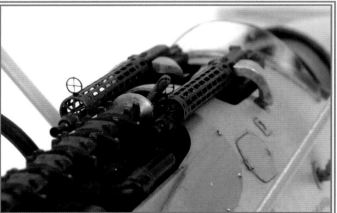

The separate and extremely fragile ring sights are fitted to the gun barrels now to avoid them being accidentally damaged.

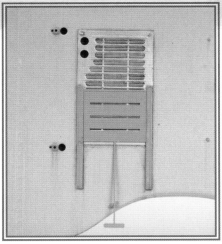

The radiator shutter is the final piece to be added before the top wing is fitted.

As usual the wing locates without any problems, however I did clumsily manage to snap the bottom pins from the outer strut on one side, meaning I had to tape the two wings together in order to repair my mistake.

Before the fun begins with the rigging I added the distinctive copper fuel pipes from the gravity fuel tank in the upper wing. These compliment the orange markings and were painted using Mr Metal Color 'Copper'.

The rigging was done using elastic EZ Line along with the superb Gaspatch turn buckles. The turnbuckles were pre-painted before starting the rigging and the lines were glued into place on the upper wing first.

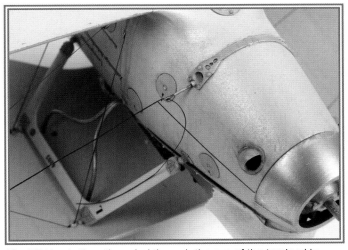

The EZ Line is then threaded through the eye of the turnbuckle, tensioned and glued in place and the excess line trimmed with a scalpel.

The other end of the turnbuckle is secured using EZ Line threaded through the pre-drilled holes in the lower wing. Once glued the excess is trimmed and any remaining holes filled.

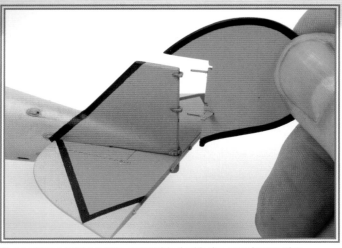

The rudder could now be assembled with the new brass pins providing a good strong assembly.

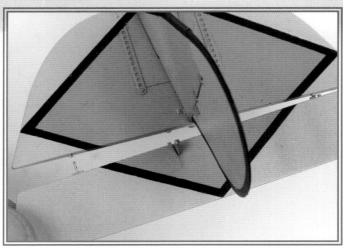

Likewise the elevator can be mounted.

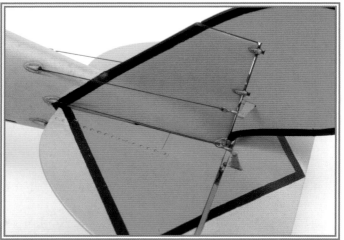

I cut down some of the Gaspatch turn buckles to fit the tail control lines. EZ Line was used again for the control cables.

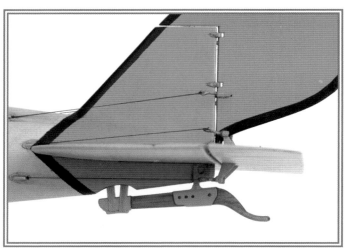

The tail skid was finished with a pale woodgrain effect.

The undercarriage, like the wings, fits perfectly and the rigging wires were added using the same techniques as for the rest of the rigging.

The wheels were treated with an acrylic wash and spattered for a used appearance.

The propeller was brush painted with two tones of brown. A wash of oil paint was then applied and grain lines painted over the base colours with the oil colour. The entire blade was then sprayed with a transparent orange to give a more varnished tone to it. Finally a layer of gloss varnish was sprayed and the decals applied. Once dry further layers of varnish were sprayed and the propeller blade was polished.

The exhaust system was painted in a grey/brown base with a mix of pink toned washes over the pipe section where they would be hottest. The lower covered section was treated differently with a hint of a metallic finish created by rubbing with some graphite powder.

D.III.a 4203/17

Since I finished my model Pheon Decals have released a set of
decals for this scheme which would have saved quite a lot of time
spent in masking the orange areas. I still think the marking
prefectly compliment the sleek lines of the Pfalz in its silver grey
factory paint.